Caernarfo
and Town Walls

Arnold Taylor **CBE, DLitt, FBA**

Wallie.

Introduction

'... to Caernarvon, where I thought to have seen a Town and a Castle, or a Castle and a Town; but I saw both to be one, and one to be both; for indeed a man can hardly divide them in judgement or apprehension; and I have seen many gallant fabrics and fortifications, but for compactness and completeness of Caernarvon, I never yet saw a parallel. And it is by Art and Nature so fitted and seated, that it stands impregnable, and if it be well manned, victualled, and ammunitioned, it is invincible, except fraud or famine do assault, or conspire against it'.

John Taylor, *A Short Relation of a Long Journey made Round or Ovall by encompassing the Principalitie of Wales, Etc.* (1652).

Opposite: Caernarfon has long been enshrined in legend and history as the fortress and palace of great rulers. King Edward I (1272–1307) was no doubt aware of its symbolic importance when he began a mighty new castle there in 1283. Perhaps it was no coincidence that in 1284, a prince, destined to become the first English prince of Wales, was born there. In this manuscript illustration, the prince — Edward of Caernarfon and later Edward II (1307–27) — is created prince of Wales by his father, King Edward I, in 1301 (British Library, Cotton Ms. Nero D II, f. 191v).

Caernarfon Castle, begun in 1283 and still not completely finished when building work stopped in about 1330, is one of the most striking buildings the Middle Ages have left to us. It is one of a group of imposing and majestic castles in north Wales that still remain in a state of some completeness. But Caernarfon undoubtedly stands apart from the others in its sheer scale, in its nobility, and in the degree of its architectural finish. Small wonder, then, that this great castle should have caught the imagination of scores of writers and painters through the ages. As early as the seventeenth century, John Taylor was clearly most impressed with the stronghold at the mouth of the Seiont river, 'by Art and Nature so fitted and seated'. Over a hundred years later, Dr Samuel Johnson (1709–84) wrote in his diary that the stupendous magnitude and strength of Caernarfon surpassed his idea, for — as he said — he did not think there had been such buildings.

From the very beginning, Caernarfon Castle was conceived as a fortress-palace of some special significance. It was to be a stronghold brimming with image and symbolism. An age-old folk memory had long associated this place with the imperial world of Rome, a tale enshrined in the well-known Macsen Wledig romance of the *Mabinogion*. King Edward I (1272–1307) chose to build on this legend. He decided to encourage his brilliant master mason and military engineer, James of St George, to build a castle that would echo the walls of the Emperor Constantine's Roman city of Constantinople. Caernarfon's 'great towers of many colours' were the crowning representation of ancient story in stone — the fairest castle that man had ever seen.

Below: The multangular towers and colour-banded walls of Caernarfon Castle, overlooking the river Seiont (Skyscan Balloon Photography for Cadw).

A History of Caernarfon Castle

Caernarfon Before King Edward I

Caernarfon is one of the historic centres of Wales, its remoter past already enshrined in legend when, just over seven hundred years ago, an English king chose it to be the seat of a new administration and gave it new fame as the cradle of a line of English princes. The castle and town walls built at that time — and still in large part surviving — were successors to a Roman fortification raised more than a thousand years earlier, the ruins of which were then to be seen standing, where their foundations may yet be seen today, on the outskirts of the town astride the way to Beddgelert. Indeed, it was from this site that Caernarfon took its name; for to the Welsh the Roman fort was *y gaer yn Arfon*, the 'stronghold in the land over against Môn' — the island of Mona or Anglesey.

A variant was *Caer Segeint*, for the name by which the Romans knew their fort was *Segontium*, from the ancient British word for the river Seiont, close to whose bank it stood. The waters of the Seiont, sheltered and tidal at this point, had much to do with its siting and carried much of its traffic.

Little can be said with certainty or precision as to the status of Caernarfon in the six and a half centuries that separate the departure of the Romans from the coming of the Normans, for history and legend are inextricably intertwined in the saga of the *Mabinogion*, in which the glory of *Segontium* is the background for historical characters in heroic guise. Apart from the sheltering haven of the Seiont itself, only one link connects that almost vanished age with

Opposite: The Roman fort of Segontium *gave its Welsh name,* y gaer yn Arfon, *to Caernarfon. The remains of the barrack blocks and the playing-card shaped defences of the fort can be clearly seen in the foreground of this aerial view. King Edward I's town and castle are in the distance, close to the shore where the river Seiont flows into the Menai Strait (Skyscan Balloon Photography for Cadw).*

Above: A gold coin of the usurper emperor, Magnus Maximus (AD 383–88), the Macsen Wledig of the Mabinogion *(National Museums & Galleries of Wales).*

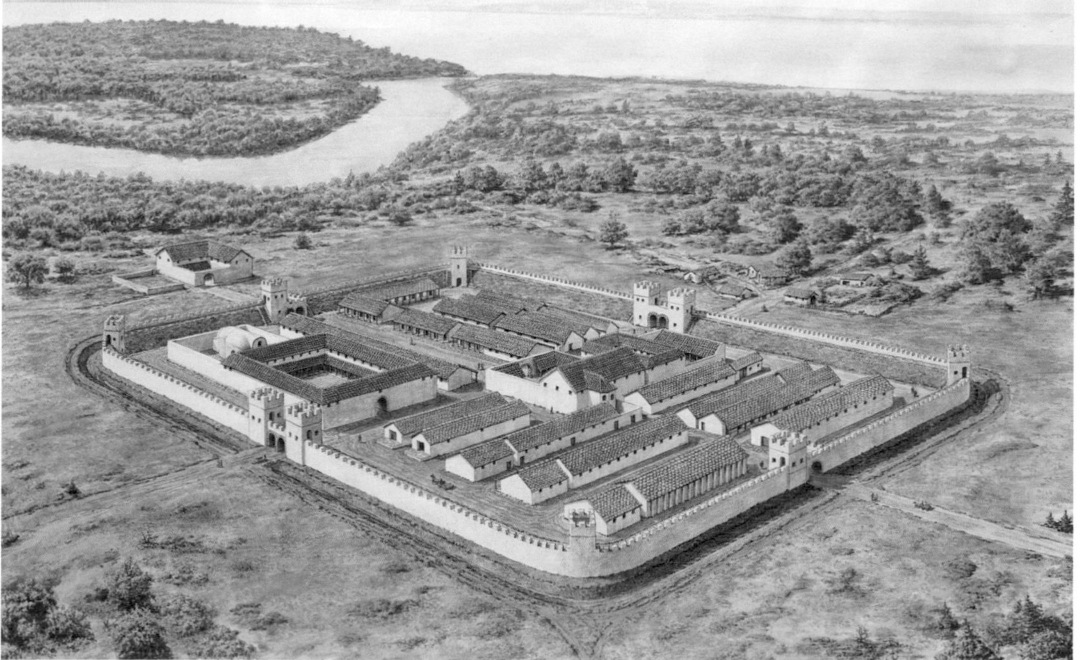

Left: An imaginative reconstruction of the Roman fort of Segontium *in about AD 250, viewed from the east. The drawing is based on archaeological excavations in 1921–23 and 1975–79 (Illustration by John Banbury 1996).*

The mother church of Caernarfon (Llanbeblig) is dedicated to St Peblig, a name derived from the Roman Publicius, reputedly a son of Magnus Maximus.

Below: An artist's impression of the motte-and-bailey castle established at Rhuddlan in 1073 by the Norman warrior, Robert of Rhuddlan. The Normans raised a similar castle at Caernarfon (Illustration by Terry Ball 1989).

later and better-known times. This is the site and dedication of Llanbeblig church, situated, not on the outskirts of medieval Caernarfon, but on Roman *Segontium*, yet continuing to this day as the mother church of the whole town. Peblig, whose name is derived from the Roman Publicius, is reputed to have been one of the sons of Magnus Maximus, emperor of Gaul, Spain and Britain from AD 383 to 388, the Macsen Wledig of the *Mabinogion*. In this church, and the buildings which preceded it, Christian worship has maintained continuity from the fifth century until our own time.

With the Norman Conquest, sealed by the coronation of William I (1066–87) at Westminster on Christmas Day 1066, we pass from obscurity to relatively well-recorded fact. The new rulers of England lost little time in seeking to bring the regions of Wales under Anglo-Norman military and political control. Already by 1073 a certain Robert, a kinsman of Hugh of Avranches (d. 1101), the first Norman

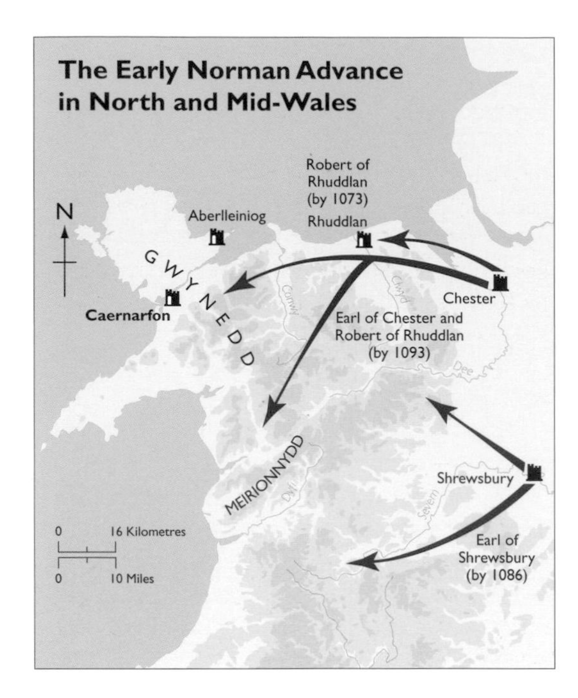

earl of Chester, had established a castle at Rhuddlan and by about 1078 had gained control of the northern coastlands up to the line of the river Conwy.

By the time of the Domesday survey (1086) this Robert of Rhuddlan — as he was called — had been granted a nominal lieutenancy over the whole of north Wales, and, together with the earl, he carried effective Norman power into Gwynedd. By 1093 castles had been established at Aberlleiniog in Anglesey, at Caernarfon, and at a site not yet certainly identified in the Welsh *cantref*, or district, of Meirionnydd.

The Normans placed their castle at Caernarfon at the water's edge, on the peninsula formed by the estuary of the Seiont, the Menai Strait and the Cadnant brook. This eleventh-century castle was of the motte-and-bailey type, with steep earthen banks and heavy timber palisading. Its dominant feature, a circular mound, or motte, was later incorporated within the upper or eastern ward of the Edwardian castle, there to survive in a modified form until after 1870. The position occupied by the Norman bailey is less certain; probably it lay to the north-east of the motte and included part of the open ground later known as the Prince's Garden and now represented by Castle Square. As to the buildings associated with the earthworks, it is likely that there would have been a tower on the mound and that at first this would have been a timber structure; but it would be unwise to assume that it necessarily remained so through the succeeding two centuries.

Nor should we suppose that no stone buildings were erected by the Welsh princes, who having recovered their losses in Gwynedd by 1115, retained possession of Caernarfon until the final collapse of native power in 1283. We know from documents dated there that Llywelyn ab Iorwerth — Llywelyn the Great (d. 1240) — sometimes resided at Caernarfon, as did his grandson Llywelyn ap Gruffudd — Llywelyn the Last (d. 1282) — later in the thirteenth century. We know, too, that around the royal court or *llys* there lay a typical Welsh *maenor*, whose territory included most of Llanbeblig with other neighbouring hamlets, and whose townsmen, with agricultural holdings in the surrounding fields, were the predecessors of the English burgesses later settled on their lands under charter from King Edward I.

The Building of the Town and Castle, First Phase: 1283–1292

In the year 1283 we enter on a new era. From this date onwards the survival of contemporary records, though but a fraction of those originally kept, enables us to follow the growth of the buildings we now see and to reconstruct the different stages of the work with reasonable confidence. Since Palm Sunday (22 March) 1282, there had been war, for the second time in five years, between King Edward I of England and Llywelyn, prince of Wales. In December 1282, Llywelyn was killed near Builth, and by 18 January the English capture of Dolwyddelan Castle, the key to Snowdonia and hub of its communications, had opened the way through the Conwy valley, the Llanberis Pass and the Vale of Ffestiniog, to Conwy, Caernarfon and Harlech.

The king himself arrived at Conwy on or about 14 March, and the construction of Conwy Castle was begun immediately. The fall of Castell y Bere

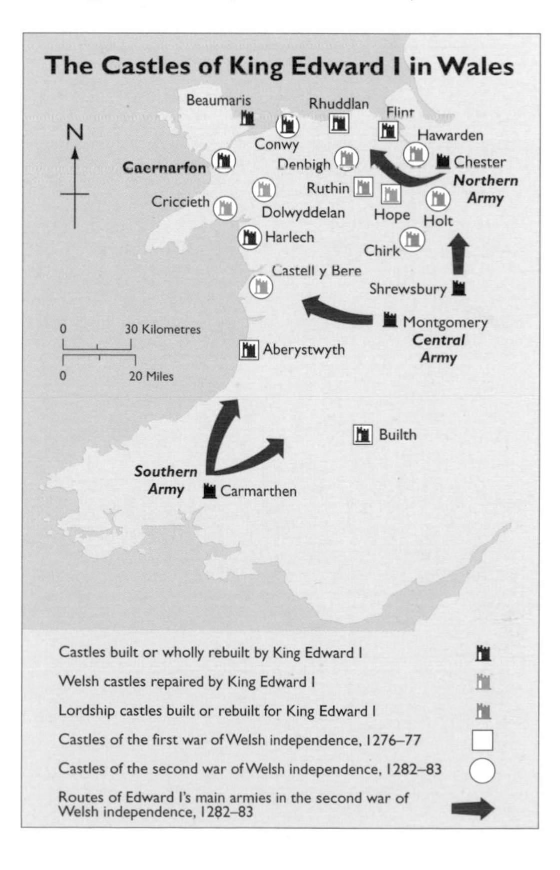

By 1115 the Welsh had recovered Caernarfon and they retained it as a royal court or llys *until 1283 during which time both Llywelyn ab Iorwerth (d. 1240) and Llywelyn ap Gruffudd (d. 1282) are known to have stayed there. This carved stone head, which may represent Llywelyn ab Iorwerth — the Great — was found at Degannwy Castle (National Museums & Galleries of Wales).*

This early fourteenth-century illustration shows a medieval king directing his master mason. The mason wears the robes of a gentleman and carries the tools of his trade — a set square and a pair of dividers (British Library, Cotton Nero, Ms. D I, f. 23v).

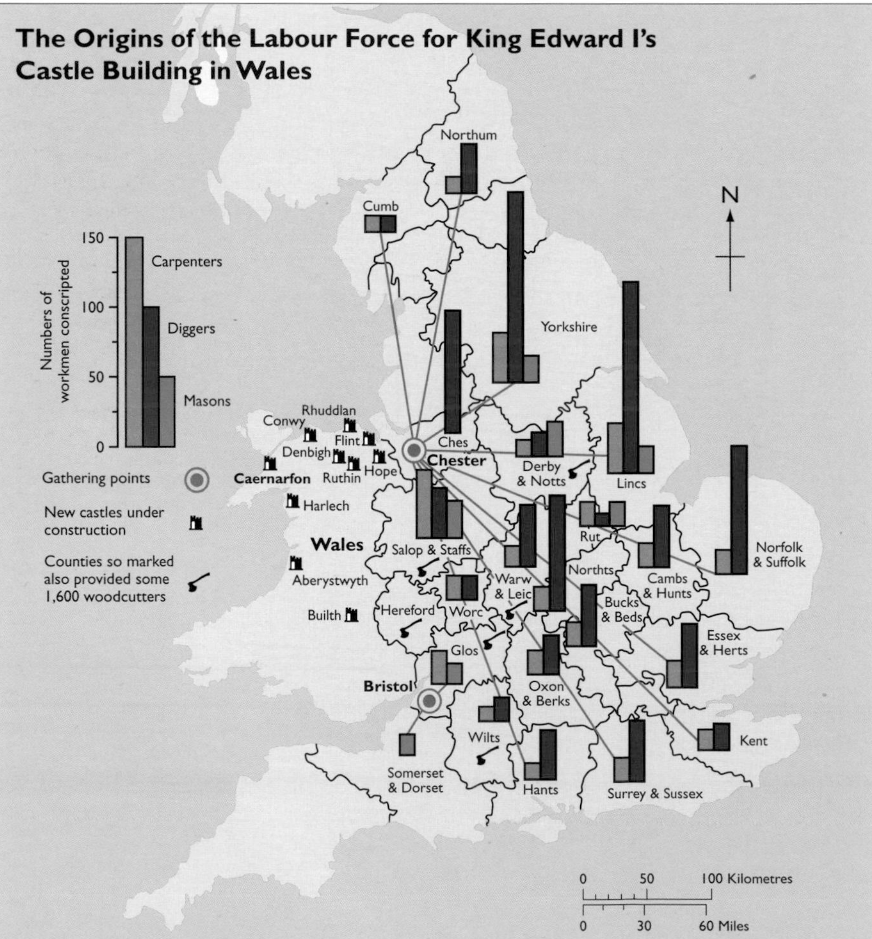

Master James of St George

Although it is difficult to assess how far such a building as Caernarfon owes its characteristic form to its designer and how far to the king and his circle, it can be said with reasonable certainty that it was James of St George (about 1235–1308) — master of the king's works in Wales — who oversaw the work at the castle. He was a highly paid master mason and military engineer whose services Edward I secured by arrangement with Count Philip of Savoy (1268–85) before March 1278. Prior to that, James had been employed successively by Count Peter II (1263–68) and Philip of Savoy as their chief household architect, in which capacity he had had at least sixteen years' experience directing castle and other works in all parts of their Alpine dominion, from the Rhône east to Turin and from Lake Neuchâtel south to beyond the Mont Cenis.

James took his surname from Philip's palace of St Georges d'Esperanche, which had been built under his direction between 1268 and 1274, and it was at St Georges that he probably resided until his transfer to Edward I's service early in 1278. He controlled, besides the works at Caernarfon, the building of Conwy, Harlech and Beaumaris, along with Flint, Rhuddlan, Aberystwyth and Builth; he also directed works at Hope in 1282 and later at Criccieth, Bere and Dolwyddelan; he may also have had at least supervisory responsibility for the castles of Denbigh, Ruthin, Holt, Hawarden and Chirk.

Master James's staff probably also included assistant masons and engineers brought from the Continent. Under this small nucleus, a veritable army of quarriers and stone-cutters, masons, smiths and carpenters, plumbers and labourers, all drawn from every shire in England and led by English masters, carried on the actual work of construction.

(north-west of Tywyn) on 25 April secured the southern flank of the English advance, while the capture of Dolbadarn, probably sometime in May, denied Llywelyn's brother, Dafydd (d. 1283), his last remaining stronghold. Within a few weeks the works begun at Conwy in March were being paralleled at Caernarfon and Harlech, and, in the years that followed, this great trio of castles, conceived on a scale which overshadowed even the might of those so recently built at Flint, Rhuddlan and Aberystwyth, rose with astonishing speed to embrace and grip the intractable heart of northern Wales.

Here we are only concerned with Caernarfon. From the beginning, the castle, the town with its wall and gates, and the quay to which most of the heavy building materials were brought by water, were pushed forward as parts of a single operation. The building of one was to some extent dependent on the building of the others. All, so far as we can now judge, were begun more or less simultaneously in the summer of 1283.

The very first recorded reference to the building works (24 June) mentions the new castle ditch, which would separate the castle from the streets and houses to the north. Next, as was done during the building of other north Wales castles, a *bretagium* or barricade was erected to fence in and protect the site of the new works. Great quantities of timber were shipped from Conwy, Rhuddlan and Liverpool, and use was also made of wood from the pontoon bridge by which, not many months earlier, an ill-starred English force had crossed from Anglesey, only to be annihilated on the Bangor shore. Diggers in their hundreds, besides excavating the castle moat, levelled platforms in the rock and cut the great foundation trenches required for walls some of which at their base are nearly 20 feet (6m) thick. Where houses of the old Welsh township lay in the way, they were demolished and their timber impounded, compensation not being paid till three years later. On the site of the future castle, substantial timber framed apartments were erected for the accommodation of King Edward and his queen, Eleanor (d. 1290). They arrived from Conwy on 11 or 12 July and stayed for more than a month before continuing their journey through Bala, Ruthin and Chester to Shrewsbury and Acton Burnell.

Preparatory work went on during the winter, and by the time Edward and Eleanor came again to Caernarfon the following Easter much progress must have been made. Indeed, it is not impossible that the Eagle Tower, which alone of all the towers can be shown to have been built complete and entire from front to rear from the first, could, if the earliest effort was concentrated on it, have already been carried up to first-floor level. If so, the tradition that it was here that the birth — on 25 April 1284 — of their son, Edward of Caernarfon, took place may indeed be a well-grounded one.

Above: A section from the accounts of payments to building workers at Caernarfon in 1284, when accommodation for the king and queen was being prepared (The National Archives: PRO, E 101/351/9).

Left: King Edward I and his queen, Eleanor (d. 1290), depicted in miniature in an illuminated initial from a fourteenth-century manuscript. They arrived at Caernarfon in July 1283 and stayed for more than a month in comfortable timber-framed apartments, amidst what must have been a busy building site. Less than a year later, they returned to the castle for the birth of their son, Edward of Caernarfon, reputedly in the partly built Eagle Tower (British Library, Cotton Nero, Ms. D II, f. 179v).

Opposite: There was considerable building activity at Caernarfon for about five years after 1283, during which time the castle would have resembled a busy building site like that shown in this late medieval German manuscript. Here, materials are being hoisted to the top of an angular tower by crane, and masons, supported on a wooden scaffold, are laying the freshly cut stone. On the ground, workmen are mixing mortar and measuring and cutting more stone (Württembergische Landesbibliothek, Stuttgart, Cod. Bibl. 2° 5, f. 9v).

By now the new moat was ready to receive its turf revetment, lime was being supplied to the castle, and stone was being ferried across from Anglesey. In this spring and summer of 1284 the castle we now see must have been beginning to take visible shape; the construction of the town walls was also progressing, and by the end of 1285 it was substantially complete. Very heavy expenditure in the 1286 building season shows that work on the castle was continuing unabated. In 1287 the high proportion of expenditure assigned to 'task', or piece, work is an indication that the chief emphasis was by that time no longer on the mass employment of masons and labourers, but rather on the 'fitting out' and on particular jobs more easily handled by smaller groups of craftsmen. In the 1288 season, works expenditure, though still appreciable, was not a tenth of what it had been. In the three following seasons it was negligible, and after 1292 the accounts cease altogether.

By this date there had been spent on the castle, town walls and related works a sum totalling approximately £12,000. This was a vast outlay, but was not disproportionate to the achievement. The town walls were probably finished, and the whole external southern façade and east end of the castle, from the Eagle Tower round to the North-East Tower, had been built to a good height. Together,

The Birth of a Prince

Right: Edward of Caernarfon was born at the castle on 25 April 1284. He was formally created prince of Wales in 1301 and acceded to the throne as King Edward II in 1307. This fourteenth-century manuscript illustration depicts the young king with his queen, Isabella (d. 1358) (The Governing Body of Christ Church, Oxford, Ms. 92, f. 4v).

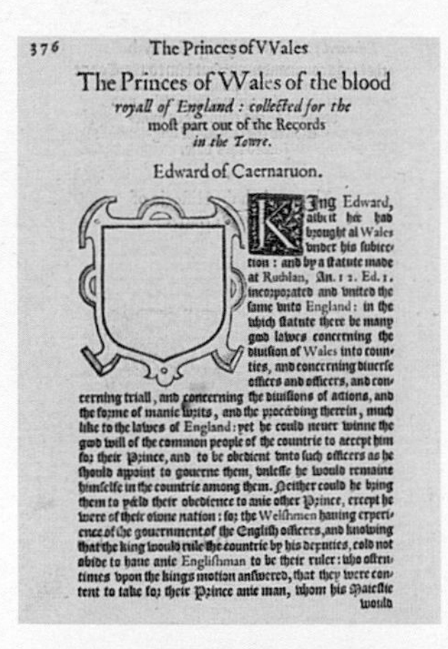

376 The Princes of VVales

The Princes of Wales of the blood
royall of England : collected for the
most part out of the Records
in the Towre.

Edward of Caernaruon.

King Edward, albeit hee had brought al Wales under his subiection: and by a statute made at Rudhlan, An. 12. Ed. 1. incorporated and united the same unto England: in the which statute there be many good lawes concerning the diuision of Wales into counties, and concerning diuerse offices and officers, and concerning triall, and concerning the diuisions of actions, and the forme of manie writs, and the proceeding therein, much like to the lawes of England: yet he could neuer winne the good will of the common people of the countrie to accept him for their Prince, and to be obedient unto such officers as he should appoint to gouerne them, unlesse he would remaine himselfe in the countrie among them. Neither could he bring them to yeeld their obedience to anie other Prince, except he were of their owne nation: for the Welshmen hauing experience of the gouernment of the English officers, and knowing that the king would rule the countrie by his deputies, cold not abide to haue anie Englishman to be their ruler: who oftentimes upon the kings motion answered, that they were content to take for their Prince anie man, whom his Maiestie would

Above: Traditionally, King Edward I presented his infant son to the people of Wales as a prince 'borne in Wales and could speake never a word of English'. David Powel's The Historie of Cambria *(1584) contains the earliest known reference to this proclamation tale (National Museums & Galleries of Wales).*

To some extent, Caernarfon's future status was determined on 25 April 1284 by the birth of a prince within the castle precincts. On his ten-year-old brother Alfonso's death four months later, the infant was to become King Edward I's eldest surviving son. It was not, however, until 1301 that Edward of Caernarfon, as he was named from his birthplace, was formally created prince of Wales and endowed with the rule and revenues of all the Crown's Welsh lands. From that date the title has normally been accorded to the eldest son of the reigning monarch.

Whether or not one of the intentions of the formal act of 1301 was to give legal effect to an earlier nomination, traditionally supposed to have been made to the Welsh nobility in the year of his birth, of a prince 'that was borne in Wales and could speake never a word of English', will perhaps never be known. The story is one that cannot be traced in writing until three hundred years later, but it is not inherently improbable and may well embody a genuine tradition. At all events, no episode is more widely associated with Caernarfon in popular thought. In 1911, when processes undreamt of in 1300 had placed among the king's chief ministers at Westminster a Welshman, namely David Lloyd George (1863–1945), elected to represent the constituency of Caernarfon Boroughs, the castle became for the first time the scene of a ceremonial royal investiture which clothed the forms and memories of the past in modern pageantry, and thereby furthered in this respect Caernarfon's claims to primacy among the towns of Wales. In 1963 Her Majesty the Queen conferred upon it the title and status of a Royal Borough, and in 1969 the investiture of Prince Charles as prince of Wales took place in the castle following the precedent established in 1911.

ls vil waz über al·

ls ich hie vor gesprochen han

ů hait die schrift uns kunt getan·

az funfzehen kunne schar

aphetes kunne gebar·

em der reine gůte man

elen unde zwentzich sune gewan·

Der ir dumheit zu rade wart··

Hic sudat Turri Babilonis·

This imaginative reconstruction depicts the Welsh assault on the town and castle of Caernarfon in September 1294, during the rebellion led by Madog ap Llywelyn. At the time of the attack, the town walls appear to have been substantially complete and the southern defences of the castle itself had probably reached a good height, creating a complete and defensible enclosure. Building work on the north face of the castle, however, does not seem to have progressed to any great extent (Illustration by Ivan Lapper 1993).

the town walls and southern face of the castle formed a complete and defensible enclosure.

Construction of the north side of the castle, which was within the covering protection of the walled town and therefore not exposed to direct attack, was less urgent. The castle was protected on this side by the great ditch hewn out at the very commencement of the work in 1283–84, a more formidable obstacle than might appear from the narrowed form in which it exists today. Consequently, as we can deduce from a contemporary record, the northern curtains had only been built to a height varying between 12 feet (3.6m) and 24 feet (7.3m) above the bottom of the ditch by the time work was about to be taken up again in the spring of 1296. By then the northern towers had also certainly been begun, but we do not know to what height they had been carried.

The 1294 Revolt and the Second Building Phase: 1294–1330

With building proceeding apace, Caernarfon's future legal and governmental roles were cast in March 1284. Under the Statute of Wales, or Rhuddlan (as it is alternatively known), among other matters of legislation, the three shires of north-west Wales — Anglesey, Caernarvon and Merioneth — were established as a single administrative unit. The new borough of Caernarfon was to be the county town of one of them, and was to serve as the centre of government for the whole.

A decade later, with building of the castle and town having reached the stage described above, the Welsh broke into widespread and open revolt. Edward I was taken completely by surprise. Almost the whole of the country was affected, with the 'national' leader, Madog ap Llywelyn, assuming the title 'prince of Wales'. Caernarfon, both the symbol and centre of the new order, was overrun, and the sheriff, one of the officers established by the Statute of 1284, was assassinated. Very heavy damage was done to the new town wall, and once this barrier had been passed little more than the wooden *bretagium* and the moat would have hindered the insurgents from swarming into the castle itself. Once they were inside, everything combustible was put to the flame. Our own narrative itself suffers from the loss of records known to have been destroyed at this time.

The king's response was swift and devastating. By the following summer, in a vigorous reaction, the English had recovered what had been lost. Orders were given for putting the town of Caernarfon in a state of defence again not later than 11 November 1295. This involved work at high pressure, and two months before the target date the rebuilding of the town walls had been completed at a cost of £1,195. This sum, nearly half the original recorded cost of the walls, shows that in places the damage must have amounted to complete destruction. This would seem to confirm that contemporary references to the town walls having been 'thrown down' by the Welsh rebels (*muri ville ... per Wallenses ... prostrati*) were not exaggerated. Next, the repair of the castle damage was taken in hand and preparations made to resume work on a major scale in the following February on the parts still unfinished.

Events had demonstrated that completion of the townward side was, after all, vital, and a document has survived suggesting that this was the section on which work was first resumed. Between July 1295 and the end of 1301 nearly £4,500 was expended on the castle works. Probably by the latter date the building up of the four lengths of curtain wall linking the Eagle and the North-East Towers had made good progress, and it is fair to presume that at least the outer faces of the intervening towers would also by this time have been carried up to an equivalent height. The vaulted passage of the King's Gate, together with its elaborate defences (pp. 22–23), and the arrowloops grouped to give maximum firepower from the curtain walls to the east, are of this period and later. All reflect the sense of insecurity left by the recent disaster.

In 1301–02 orders were given to rebuild in stone the wooden bridge by which, prior to 1294, the main gate of the town had been approached across the Cadnant (pp. 41–42). Then, between November 1301 and September 1304, there is a gap in the accounts. This may mean that building at the castle had been largely brought to a standstill by the transfer of labour to the war in Scotland. Walter of Hereford, the master mason who had had charge of the works since 1295, was certainly in Scotland during the years in question, but after Edward's victory at Stirling in 1304 it was possible to take up work once again on the unfinished buildings at Caernarfon.

Work was resumed in the autumn of 1304 and we know that approximately £700 was spent in each of the next two years. Expenditure of this order allowed the employment of 70 to 100 men in the winter months and 150 to 200 in the summer. Though details are lacking, there is no reason to suppose that progress was not maintained at something like this level through the three following years also. From 1309 until 1330, and very possibly for a few years longer, building went steadily on, but on nothing like the scale reached in the 1280s and after the 1294 revolt. Proportionately to the whole building, we should expect to assign relatively little new construction to these final years, and there are documents which help us to say what it was.

In 1316 the timber-framed 'Hall of Llywelyn', part of the last Welsh prince's residence at Conwy, was dismantled and shipped to Caernarfon, where it was re-erected within the castle. In 1317 the Eagle Tower was nearing completion, and a carved stone eagle was being affixed on it. There is evidence in the

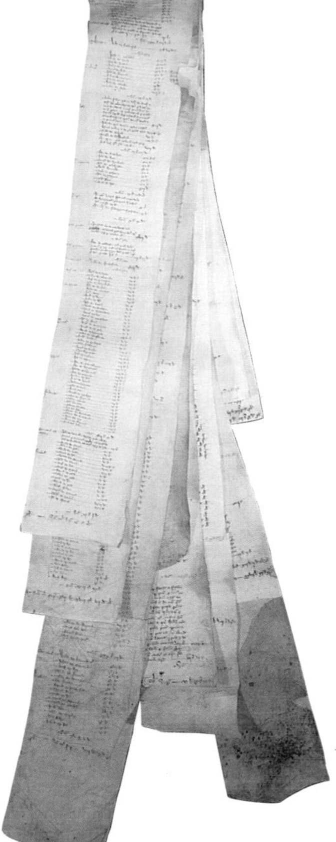

For parts of the year 1316–17, week-by-week particulars recorded on parchment rolls survive to provide a vivid picture of the building efforts during the latter stages of construction at Caernarfon. The enlarged section shown below records payments to Robert the Smith who received 14d. for making 140 roof nails, 140 clench nails, and for mending tools. He was also to prepare three iron cramps for fixing a stone eagle on the 'great tower' — the Eagle Tower (The National Archives: PRO, E 101/486/29).

building itself that in the 1280s the tower had been left with a temporary roof at what ultimately became the level of its top floor. The addition of the fourth storey and the three turrets — all no doubt envisaged in the original plans — was a major task, and must have accounted for a high proportion of the later expenditure. Another piece of work belonging to this period is the upper part of the curtain wall linking the Eagle and the Queen's Towers. A third is the upper portion of the King's Gate. We learn from the accounts that the statue of Edward of Caernarfon — by this time King Edward II (1307–27) — was being erected here in 1320. In the same year oak beams 32 feet (9.6m) long, from the woods in the Conwy valley, were being obtained to floor the hall above the gate. Probably one of the last works undertaken was the rearward extension of the western gate tower; this was apparently designed to be the first instalment of a scheme which, if completed, would virtually have trebled the defences of the entrance, with subsidiary gates and portcullises opening east and west towards the respective baileys from a central octagonal space. That more of it was built than now remains is almost certain.

Speaking broadly, by 1330, when regular building payments cease to be recorded, the structure of the castle had been carried to much the state in which we see it today. Subsequent works of which we have record were of no more than a minor character. The total expenditure from 1283 onwards had been from £20,000 to £25,000, its outlay being spread over nearly fifty years. It includes the cost of building not only the castle itself, but also the town wall with its gates, towers and multi-arched bridge approach, the quay and other works, as well as the extensive reparations made necessary by the damage of Madog's rising and of an accidental fire which swept the town in 1304. Even so, much that was planned in the castle was never undertaken.

The Queen's Gate, the outer façade of which was almost certainly completed in the 1280s, was left unfinished at the back. The toothing on the North-East and Granary Towers is an indication of unbuilt wings, two storeys high, against the adjacent curtain walls. A massive foundation, projecting inwards from the wall between the Black and Chamberlain Towers, suggests that it was proposed to enclose this side of the Norman mound with a wall which would probably have connected with buildings at the back of the King's Gate.

Opposite: The Eagle Tower, perhaps the crowning glory of Caernarfon, was finally nearing completion in 1317, when a carved stone eagle was affixed to it. Work had commenced here in earnest from 1283 but later in the 1280s it seems that the tower was provided with a temporary roof following the completion of the first three storeys.

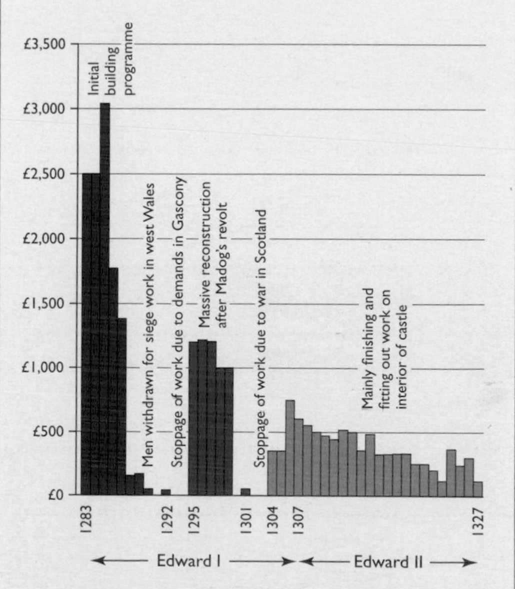

Far left: Part of the tomb effigy of King Edward II in Gloucester Cathedral. In 1320, a statue of the king was being erected in the niche above the King's Gate at Caernarfon (Conway Library, Courtauld Institute of Art).

By 1330, when building ceased at Caernarfon, construction had been in progress for a period of almost fifty years and the town and castle had reached their maximum extent. Although parts of the castle were to remain forever incomplete and it was to suffer decay and depredation, in 1538 the walls were then, as now, 'exceeding good'. This artist's view of Caernarfon shows the borough, quay and castle as they may have appeared when building work stopped in the early fourteenth century (Illustration by Ivan Lapper 1993).

Later History

For two hundred years the political arrangements established by the Statute of Wales in 1284 remained in force, and walled towns such as Caernarfon continued to be closed to all but English burgesses. The accession to the English throne, in 1485, of a king of Welsh lineage, in the person of Henry Tudor — King Henry VII (1485–1509) — opened the way to concessions in this respect to the Welsh-speaking population. Fifty years later, this also led to a measure of assimilation of the governmental system of Wales to that of England. Until the time of these changes, the castle continued to be maintained and garrisoned, and successfully withstood sieges by Owain Glyn Dŵr and his French allies in 1403 and 1404. Town and castle together formed the effective capital of north Wales, providing at once a safe residence for government officials and a centre for their activities.

Tudor rule, by softening old hostilities and promoting peaceful intercourse with England, diminished the need for English castles in Wales. From the sixteenth century onwards, therefore, these great buildings were increasingly neglected, and in 1538 Caernarfon, with the rest, was reported as 'moche ruynous and ferre in decaye for lakke of tymely reparations'.

The walls, then as now, were 'exceeding good', but the lead work on the roofs of several of the towers had seen no major renewal for centuries; it had resulted in rotten timbers crashing through the floors below. In 1620, only the Eagle Tower and the King's Gate were still roofed and leaded, the ground-floor rooms on either side of the latter having long been used as county prisons, the one for felons and the other for debtors. As for the buildings within the castle, they were 'all quite faln down to the ground and the Tymber and the rest of the materialls as Iron and Glasse carryed away and nothing left that [is] valiable'.

Such was the condition of a building which, in the Civil War (1642–48), was once more garrisoned for the king and thrice besieged. But to external appearance little was amiss, and after the war, as before it, a sensitive observer could not but be enraptured by the strength and perfection of the fortifications. There were others, however, who only saw them as a source of trouble, and in 1660 the government ordered the castle and town walls to be dismantled and demolished at the expense of the county, the cost to be defrayed as far as possible from the sale of the materials. Local authority readily agreed, 'conceiving it to be for the great advantage of ourselves and posterity to have the Castle of Caernarvon and the strengthes thereof demolished'. Perhaps the 'strengthes thereof' prevailed, for demolition, if indeed it was ever started, cannot have proceeded far, and posterity is still happily free to decide whether the destruction of a monument of a grandeur unsurpassed in Wales, if not in Britain, would after all have been so greatly to its advantage.

Caernarfon having thus escaped disaster, the eighteenth-century engravers, such as the brothers Buck (1742) and John Boydell of Hawarden (1750), were able to take pleasure in depicting a town and castle whose site, character and setting had in essentials scarcely altered from their foundation. The change to

Left: John, first Lord Byron (d. 1652) — the last fighting constable of Caernarfon. The castle was garrisoned for King Charles I during the Civil War of 1642–48, and it was Byron who finally surrendered it to the parliamentarians in 1646 (Tabley House Collection, University of Manchester/ Bridgeman Art Library).

Below: In the eighteenth century, Caernarfon began to attract the interest of artists, including the Buck brothers and John Boydell of Hawarden. J. M. W. Turner (1775–1851) visited the town in 1798 and again in 1799, though it was not until 1833 that he completed this magnificent watercolour of the castle, suffused with the gentle, muted tones typical of his later work (British Museum, London, 1958-7-12-439).

An 1843 poster in which a Caernarfon shipowner offers emigrants a chance to sail direct to the United States of America in his barque, the Hindoo, *with a ballast of slates (Caernarfon Public Library).*

modern conditions did not set in till the very end of the century. New roads, the first since Roman days, were built, and the north Wales slate industry was then expanding to serve both home and overseas markets.

Hitherto unknown prosperity came to the port in 1827–28. It was at this time that George (1781–1848) and Robert Stephenson (1803–59) constructed a narrow-gauge railway to bring to the new 'slate quay' below the castle the products of the Gloddfarlon quarries at Nantlle, 10 miles (16km) away. The slate trade, more than any other single factor, accounted for a rise in Caernarfon's population from less than 4,000 in 1801 to nigh on 9,000 in 1851. In 1843 a local shipowner, with offices in the High Street, was even inviting emigrants to sail direct from Caernarfon to New York in his fast 600-ton sailing barque *Hindoo*, 'with a ballast of slates'. In 1852 the town was connected by standard-gauge railway to the main London, Chester and Holyhead line; this meant further expansion of the slate trade, while for Caernarfon itself the new means of communication marked the end of the era of isolation and self-sufficiency.

It was at this time of growing contact with a world beyond the limits of north Wales that the castle began to be rescued from the neglect of

Below: Hitherto unknown prosperity came to the port of Caernarfon in the early nineteenth century. It was in 1827–28 that a narrow-gauge railway linked the new 'slate quay', seen in this lithograph of 1830, to the nearby Gloddfarlon slate quarries at Nantlle (Llyfrgell Genedlaethol Cymru/ National Library of Wales).

centuries, and a programme of repairs undertaken at government expense. The work thus begun was pursued with vigour in the last thirty years of the nineteenth century under the direction of the deputy-constable, Sir Llewelyn Turner (1823–1903). He renewed the stone steps and newels in several of the towers, restored battlements, repaired the Chamberlain Tower, completed the top of the Well Tower, floored and roofed the Queen's Tower, and — in the teeth of local opposition — cleared out the northern moat and removed a clutter of unsightly encroachments from against the outer walls.

Turner's new ashlar work is readily distinguishable by the buff colour and fine grain of the material employed, a sandstone from the neighbourhood of Mostyn in Flintshire. The appearance of the castle today owes much to his vision and pertinacity.

In 1908 control of the castle, which has always remained the property of the Crown, was transferred from the Office of Woods and Forests (which had become the responsible department in 1832) to the Office of Works. Since then it has been maintained as a historic building under the supervision of the Ancient Monuments Branch of that Office and its successors. The duties are currently the responsibility of Cadw, the historic environment service of the Welsh Government.

Further repairs were undertaken in connection with the investiture ceremony in 1911, and the massive ceilings in the principal towers, following the evidence of those that had been there originally, are of this period. The town walls, having become annexed to and, for much of their length, obscured by the various properties built against them (for the most part in the early years of the nineteenth century), have also been opened up again. Their clearance was completed in 1963, and they are now treated as a monument deserving the same care and appreciation as the castle.

In 1986, Caernarfon Castle and the town walls were inscribed on the World Heritage List as a historic site of outstanding universal value.

Top left: Under the direction of Sir Llewelyn Turner (1823–1903), who served as deputy-constable of Caernarfon in the late nineteenth century, the castle began to be rescued from centuries of neglect.

Above: The construction of seating formed part of the preparations for the investiture of Prince Edward at Caernarfon Castle in 1911. The ceremony also prompted further repairs to the medieval masonry.

A Tour of Caernarfon Castle

This tour will take you around the castle and town walls, describing the main features of interest. It is not essential to follow the route as set out, and you may prefer to make your own way around using the 'bird's-eye view' at the front of the guide or the plan shown here.

This particular tour of the castle, however, starts at the main entrance to the site (the King's Gate), and guides you around the interior in an anti-clockwise direction. We will visit each of the towers in turn, eventually returning to the point of departure.

When you leave the castle, you may wish to turn right for the circuit of the town walls, ending up at the castle car park by the river. Or, if preferred, you can turn left and return direct to the car park.

Several of the towers contain exhibitions and there is also an audio-visual presentation in the theatre on the first floor of the Eagle Tower. You may also wish to visit the Museum of the Royal Welch Fusiliers housed in the Queen's Tower and Chamberlain Tower and the intervening upper wall-passage.

The Castle Plan

The plan of the castle is shaped rather like a 'figure eight', originally divided into two at the waist with a lower ward to the right (west) of the main entrance and an upper ward to the left (east). In general terms, towers and connecting curtain walls survive largely complete, albeit with some restoration at the wall heads, and with timber floors inserted in the larger towers around 1911.

The courtyard buildings, however, have disappeared except for foundations or toothing projecting from the curtain walls. Some of the buildings, such as the back parts of the Queen's Gate, and perhaps of the King's Gate, were probably never completed, while others, such as the kitchens, may not have been built as originally intended, or were never built at all.

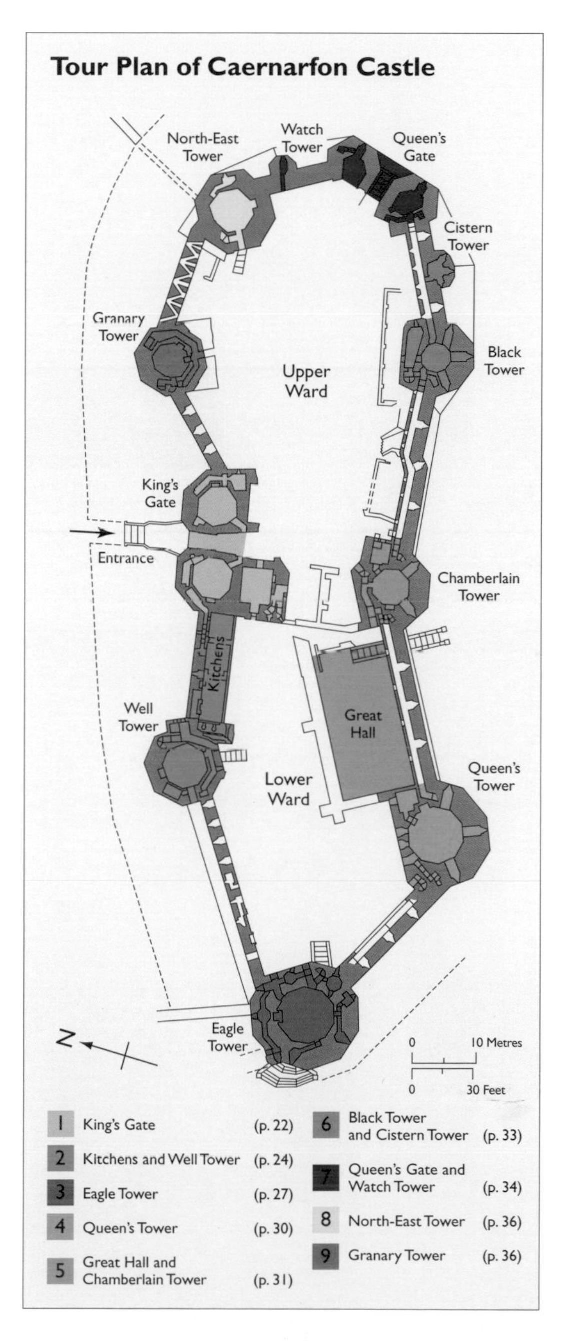

Opposite: The overall plan of Caernarfon is shaped like a figure eight, divided into two wards at the waist. In this view from the Eagle Tower, looking along the full length of the interior of the castle, the lower ward is in the foreground, the narrower waist at the centre and the upper ward beyond.

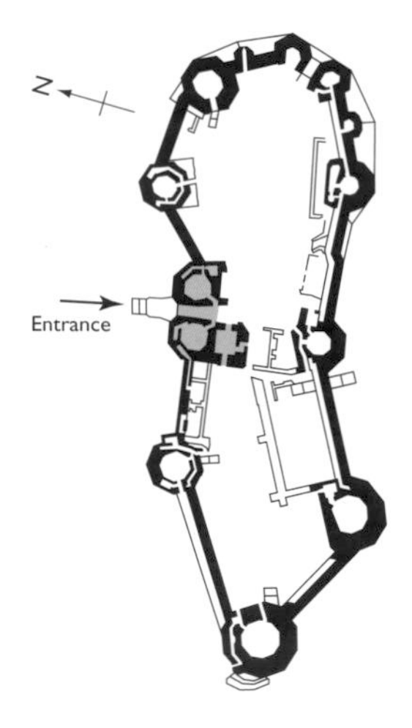

The King's Gate is perhaps the most striking demonstration of the strength of medieval fortification in the British Isles.

The King's Gate

No building in Britain demonstrates more strikingly the immense strength of medieval fortification than the great twin-towered gateway to Caernarfon Castle. Had the gatehouse been fully completed, intruders would have had to cross a drawbridge, pass through five doors and under six portcullises, with a right-angled turn as they passed from the main gate-passage to a smaller passage, along the south side of the gatehouse, before entering the lower ward over a second drawbridge. Arrowloops and spy holes flank and command the approach from different levels, while in the vaulting above there are groups of 'murder holes' to threaten assailants, and from which water could be poured down to extinguish any fire that might be started against the gates. Evidence for all these features is preserved in the walls, although the main bridge pit and its bearings are concealed by the modern wooden decking. Beyond the line of the third portcullis, doors on either side lead to the porters' rooms.

As you leave the gatehouse passage turn right towards the lower ward. On the wall to your right (at the back of the shop), you will see the vertical grooves for portcullises [**1**], the springing of the vault over this smaller passage [**2**], and the holes in the wall which mark the position of the gudgeon pins from which the wooden gates were suspended.

Near here is the access to the upper part of the gatehouse. A door on the right opens to a stair in the rearward part of the building [**3**]. This leads up to a wall-passage at first-floor level from which there is a modern footbridge across the north-west gate tower to the room above the main gate-passage [**4**]. Here a double piscina or sink in the east wall shows

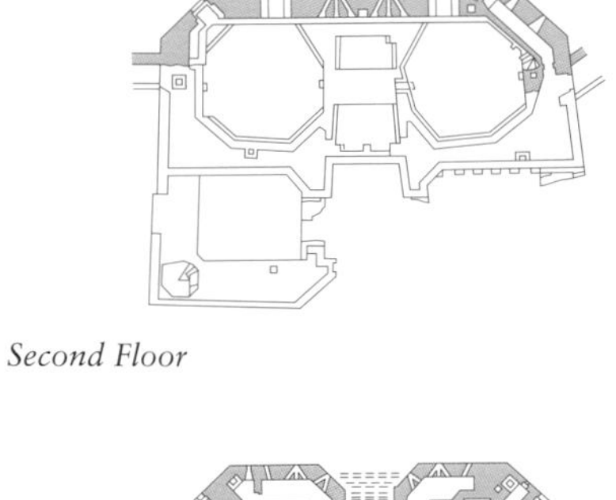

Second Floor

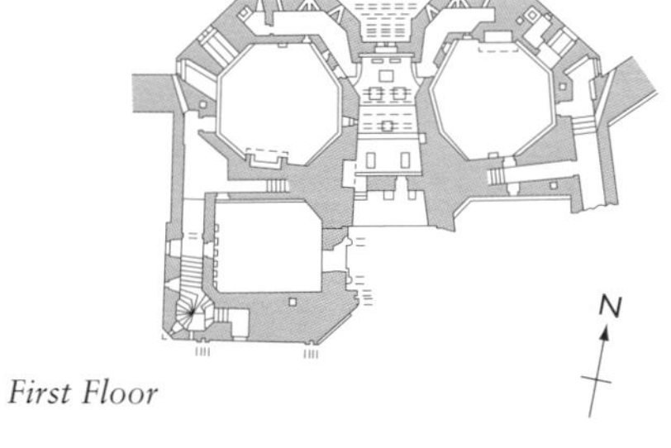

First Floor

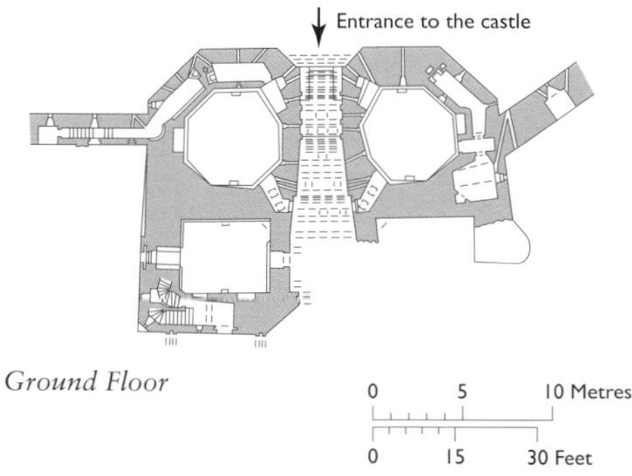

Ground Floor

that this was a chapel, though because of its position not on the normal east–west orientation. Two of the portcullises rose up through the chapel floor, demonstrating that in a medieval castle the great gate was seldom open and then only for the briefest interval. The wall-passages at this level contain, in addition to a latrine to the left, arrowloops grouped in such a way that although only six openings are apparent from outside the castle, double that number of archers could discharge their shafts through them simultaneously.

Above the chapel, and the room in the tower on either side, there was to have been a large hall, 60 feet (18m) long [**5**]. The principal features of its north wall, apparently the only part to be completed, are three large two-light windows with seats [**6**], and over the gate two more groups of three-in-one arrowloops [**7**]. The projecting stone corbels for the roof supports are carved with what were once finely decorated heads [**8**]. Having observed these features, you should now return to ground level.

Details at the back of the King's Gate, such as the 'toothing' marking the positions of unfinished walls, indicate that the gate was probably never completed. The numbers refer to the main points of interest discussed in the text.

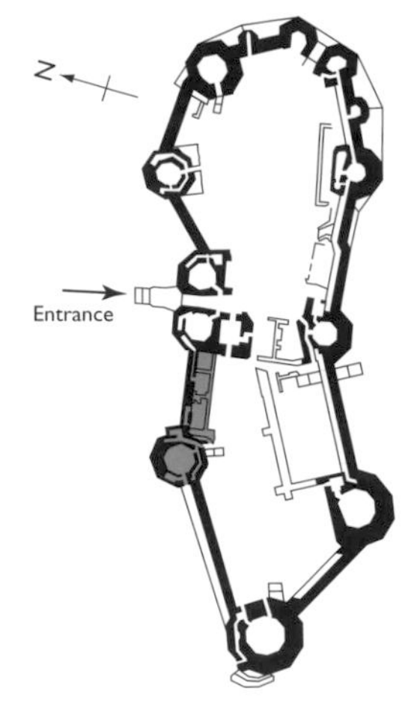

The kitchen area — conveniently located adjacent to the Well Tower and opposite the great hall — was probably never completed or used as originally intended. The seatings for copper cauldrons at the west (left) end of the range indicate the planned position of the boiling house. Here, meat would have been boiled and the remaining stock used to make pottage — a soup-like dish that was a staple part of the medieval diet.

The Kitchens

To the west (right) of the King's Gate lies the lower ward. Note the foundations of the broad wall that was intended to separate the two wards. Around the enclosing curtain walls, you will also see the foundations of the buildings which formerly occupied the ward; they would have concealed the lower parts of the curtain itself.

As you walk down towards the Eagle Tower you will come first, on your right, to the site of the castle kitchens, lying between the gatehouse and the Well Tower. The springer of a great arch and bonding for a cross partition wall, both built as part of the curtain wall, show that it was intended to build the whole in stone. But the slight foundation walls on the courtyard side suggest that, as built, these kitchens may have been relatively flimsy structures.

To the left of the range of rooms are the remains of settings for two copper cauldrons, with fireplaces below them [1]. This was intended to be the boiling house, and the toothing [2] for the huge stone chimney above the cauldrons can be seen in the curtain wall, though it may never have been completed as planned. Behind them, in the thickness of the tower wall, is a cavity which could have been used for storing dry foods such as spices [3]. At the bottom of the wall, on the right-hand side of this cavity, there is a small hole [4] marking the end of a water channel running from a tank in the Well Tower, and below it there is a drain running off to the left [5].

The main kitchen [6] as planned would have been located to the right of the boiling house and the thick partition wall — the toothing for which is clear on the curtain wall — would probably have contained a large fireplace within its thickness [7]. Access between the boiling house and the kitchen was by way of a short wall-passage [8] in which there is the line of a second channel, still bearing the remains of its lead piping, running from the Well Tower to a stone sink, now much weathered, mounted in a recess in the wall about the middle of the range [9]. In the wall below the great stone springer [10], on the right, is the small opening for a rubbish disposal shaft in the wall thickness [11].

The accommodation at the right-hand end of these apartments was of two storeys [12]; a doorway in the curtain wall opens on to a stair which served the upper room and the gatehouse.

The Well Tower

There are two entrances to the Well Tower from the courtyard, one at ground level, and the other leading into the basement. First, descend the steps to the latter, noting on the way down the position of the door which originally barred the entry. From the basement it is possible to obtain a 'cross-section' view of what was involved in the construction of all the ten major towers of the castle, for here none of the timber floors of the upper storeys have been restored, allowing the characteristic details of each room to be seen at a glance from below.

Including the basement, there were in all four storeys, and this was so in the majority of the northern towers. At basement level there is a wide gateway, once defended with outer and inner doors, portcullis and 'murder holes'. This gateway was originally designed to allow water-borne supplies for the adjacent kitchens and service rooms to be brought in from the ditch (p. 44). At each of the three upper levels there is a pair of square holes on opposite sides of the tower, which, with supporting corbels below, carried the great cross-beams on which were laid the joists of the main floors. Each of these upper rooms has its own fireplace and its latrine reached by a passage in the thickness of the outside wall, arrangements which are common to practically all the rooms in the castle. The tower was left unfinished in the fourteenth century and much of its top, including the whole of the surmounting turret, is nineteenth-century work (p. 19).

Return to ground level and re-enter the tower by the entrance near the top of the basement steps. From here a passage leads to the chamber containing the well which gives the tower its name; the well itself being almost 50 feet (15m) deep. Facing the well is a stone seating for a lead-lined cistern, which could be kept filled by buckets raised from the well, and from which ran inclined pipes in the thickness of the wall to the kitchens nearby. The well shaft extends upwards, also allowing the water to be drawn at first-floor level.

Next to the well chamber, winding steps lead to the upper levels. At first-floor level, above the well chamber, there is a small room with a fireplace,

The ground-floor entrance to the Well Tower leads to the well chamber itself, seen to the right of this view. The well, covered by the modern grille, is nearly 50 feet (15m) deep.

possibly a little private kitchen. Also at this level, there is a wall-walk westwards to the Eagle Tower.

At the second-floor level there is a doorway intended to lead on to an upper wall-walk towards the Eagle Tower, but the curtain wall at this point was never carried above the first-floor stage. From the second-floor vestibule, steps lead up eastwards to the wall-walk on that side. At present, it can be followed at this level across the King's Gate, through the intervening towers, all the way to the North-East Tower. Finally, a newel staircase from the second-floor level also leads up to the restored battlements and the tower's surmounting turret.

Back at ground level, you will see signs of a range of rooms against the curtain wall between the Well Tower and Eagle Tower. There is a restored fireplace, roof corbels and partition bonding stones representing these rooms. They were possibly never completed, or perhaps built with timber-framed walls.

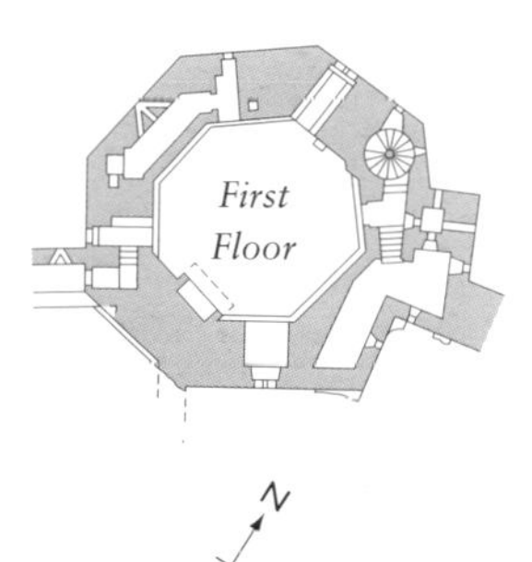

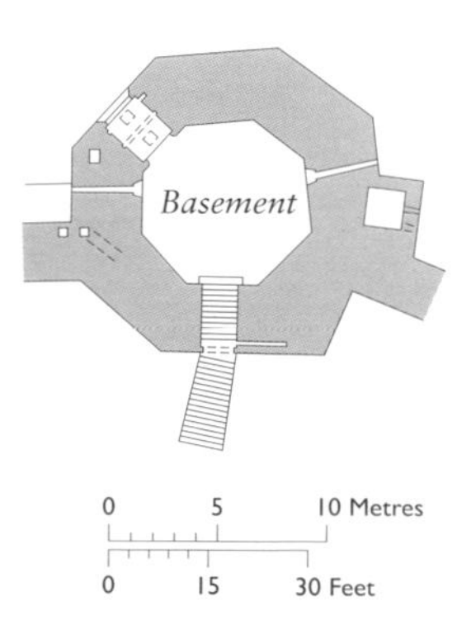

Food and Cooking

Peter Brears

Providing the food for a great castle-palace such as Caernarfon was a massive undertaking. In the early fourteenth century the kitchens might have had to feed a royal household of around 350 servants, 200 builders and the permanent garrison — a total of perhaps 600 people every day. As originally planned, but never completed, it was intended that supplies would be shipped into a dock just outside the Well Tower, and there unloaded directly into the tower's large basement store room. The gateway here was strongly defended by two pairs of doors and a portcullis. A stair wide enough for two porters to pass led up to the lower ward, where the granaries and larders were probably located.

Right: The settings for two copper cauldrons, with fireplaces below them, at the west end of the kitchen range mark the intended position of the boiling house.

Below: A cutaway reconstruction drawing to show how the boiling house, kitchen and Well Tower may have been used had the buildings been completed as planned (Illustration by Chris Jones-Jenkins 2004).

The ground floor of the Well Tower was ideally placed to serve as the counting house — the central finance office of the royal household. This was controlled by three high-ranking officers: the steward, the treasurer and the controller, assisted by the cofferer, who collected the required funds and provided the money for purchases, and a number of clerks. Meeting here every morning they would make up their accounts and then go out to supervise the issue of food from the stores and inspect the food that was served into the hall and elsewhere. As fresh supplies were delivered, their quantity, quality and price were recorded from which a cost per meal could be calculated. At the end of the day records of the food issued and meals served were compared and the cooks who could not explain any losses subjected to substantial fines. The deep window recess in this room, lined with stone benches, would have made an ideal carrel for writing up the records in an otherwise gloomy room.

Boiled meat formed a large part of the diet and the room east of the Well Tower was a boiling house equipped with two stone 'furnaces'. Flames from their wood fires heated the two huge copper boiling pans supported above by strong iron stands. An adjacent window provided the necessary illumination and a huge chimney above carried off the smoke and steam. Water for the boilers was probably supplied by pipe from the Well Tower, a further pipe filling a cistern in the main kitchen beyond, where most of the food for the great hall was cooked.

All of the king's meals were prepared separately by his personal cooks, including one who concentrated on his breakfast. For convenience and security a privy kitchen was included in a top-floor wall chamber in the Eagle Tower — this presumably being an interim measure as major royal apartments were planned to be built elsewhere.

The Eagle Tower

This is the greatest of all the castle's towers and was probably at first intended to provide accommodation for Sir Otto de Grandison, the king's lieutenant and first justiciar of north Wales. Everything about it is designed on a magnificent scale. Like the other northern towers it comprises a basement and three storeys, but there is more generous provision of wall-chambers and its group of three lofty turrets gives it special distinction.

The basement forms an antechamber through which anyone coming to Caernarfon by water would enter the castle. We, however, enter it by the steps leading down from the courtyard. The basement, like the three great rooms above, is ten-sided and measures some 30 to 35 feet (9 to 10.5m) across.

On the side opposite the entrance steps there is the passage leading in, through a portcullis and strongly barred double door, from the waterside. From this passage, there are stairs communicating with the intended Water Gate (see p. 44). Another passage from the chamber would have given access to the basement of the buildings against the north curtain wall. With all the doors closed, the only natural light to come into the room would have been provided by a tall, single arrowloop at the face of a deep embrasure. At this point we can see the immense thickness of the tower walls, here about 18 feet (5.4m). A passage at one side of the embrasure led to a latrine.

The ground-floor room in the Eagle Tower is approached through a vestibule from the courtyard. Though dark, it is a room of noble proportions (at present occupied by an exhibition), and it is fitted with a large hooded fireplace. The floor and ceiling (the latter a close replica of the original arrangement) date from 1911–14, as do those elsewhere. Doors lead from this main chamber to passages and subsidiary chambers in the thickness of the walls. The little chamber opposite the entrance contained the gear for raising the portcullis of the postern gate below, while the passage to the right would have led to a room serving the same purpose over the adjacent Water Gate.

To the left of the entrance vestibule is the stair to the upper floors and close to its foot

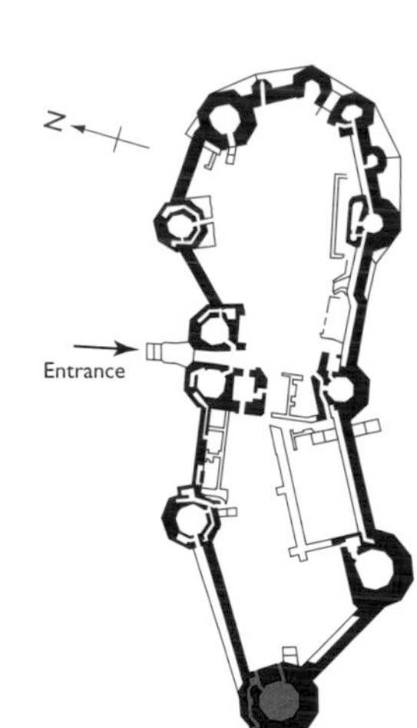

A cutaway drawing of the Eagle Tower from the north-east, showing the internal arrangement of the rooms and wall-passages (Illustration by Chris Jones-Jenkins 1996).

The small first-floor room traditionally, but almost certainly incorrectly, identified as the birthplace of Edward of Caernarfon (later King Edward II).

The much-weathered remains of a stone eagle on the battlements of the west turret of the Eagle Tower.

Opposite: Everything about the Eagle Tower was designed on a magnificent scale. Its grand proportions set it apart from all the other towers in the castle. From the outset, it was probably intended to provide accommodation for King Edward I's lieutenant in north Wales, Sir Otto de Grandison (1238–1328).

is a small octagonal chamber which was probably a chapel. The same arrangement occurs in similarly placed rooms in the Queen's and Chamberlain Towers.

The main chamber on the first floor, which currently houses a theatre, was originally the principal apartment of the tower and is like that below but better lit. There is the same elaborate provision of accommodation in the thickness of the walls, with the south-east angle occupied, as on the floor below, by an octagonal chapel; here the purpose is made certain by the remains of a trefoil-headed piscina — a sink for holy water. To the right of the entrance vestibule, a passage leads to a small rectangular room traditionally, but almost certainly wrongly, identified as the birthplace of the first English prince of Wales. If, by the time of his birth in April 1284, the walls of the Eagle Tower had been built to this height, the main chamber would surely be the more likely location. Inserted in the window of the small room are the arms of Albert Edward, prince of Wales, afterwards King Edward VII (1901–10). For a time at least the tower did not extend above this level, the second floor and watch towers above being fourteenth-century additions. The evidence for this is the up-and-down slope of the offset in the central chamber where the ceiling rests on the walls showing that they were first built to take a low-pitched outer roof at this point.

The topmost room, entered directly from the stair, is well lit by a pair of two-light windows, both with stepped window-seats, and there is a large fireplace. There are rectangular wall chambers on the north (accessed from the northern window embrasure) and north-east (accessed from the stair), the latter is perhaps a kitchen, while a passage on the south leads to a latrine.

The main stair leads on up to the roof of the tower, and from here to the top of the most westerly of the three turrets. The battlements, both on the tower and on the turrets, are unrestored, and their copings preserve the remains of the numerous stone figures with which they were originally decorated. Some of these were evidently helmeted heads, while on the west turret an eagle — although much weathered — is still recognizable. Remains of similar stone figures will be noticed in other parts of the castle.

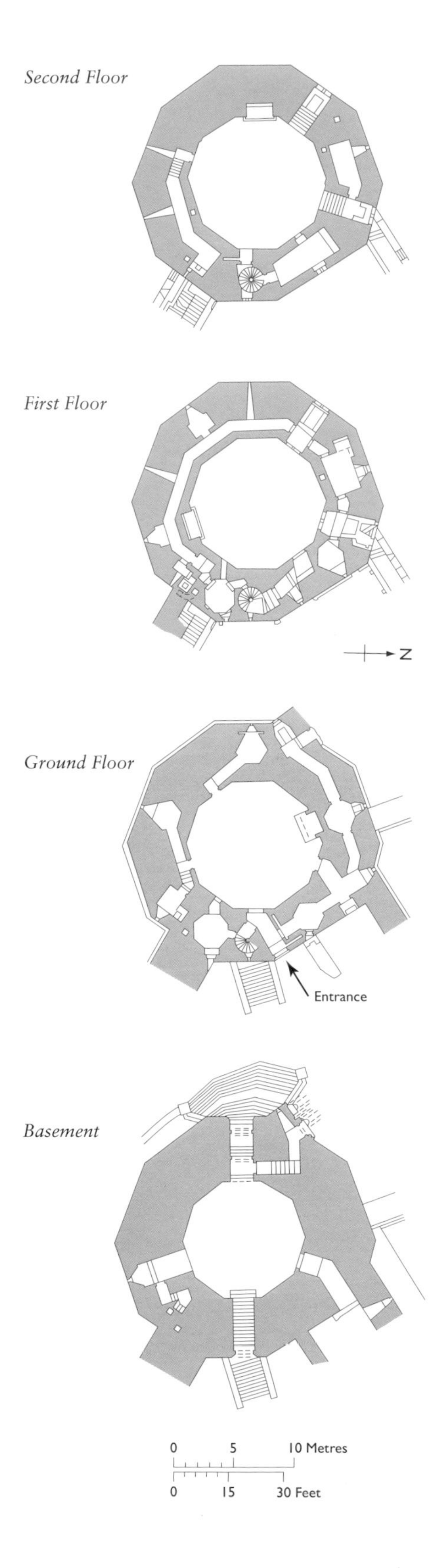

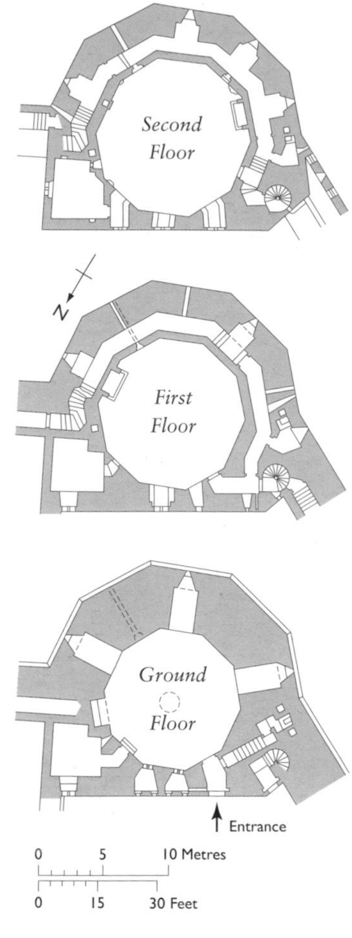

The Queen's Tower

The regimental museum of the Royal Welch Fusiliers now occupies the Queen's Tower and two floors of the Chamberlain Tower. The museum is entered from the ground floor of the Chamberlain Tower and information panels in the upper wall-passage, accessed from the first-floor chamber, lead the visitor through a 'one-way' circuit to further displays in the Queen's Tower.

The Queen's Tower is linked to the Eagle Tower by a length of curtain with wall-walks at two levels, the lower evidently intended to be completed as a covered passage like those further to the east. Against this wall there has been a building of which only foundations survive. The two towers have common internal dimensions and wall thicknesses, but here there are only three storeys. On the right, at the north-west corner of the tower, there is a spiral stair from the courtyard to the roof, which communicated with the two upper rooms and their encircling wall-passages. The wall-walk, accessible from the roof of the tower, and the lower wall-passage can be followed the full length of the south curtain to the Queen's Gate. Each floor also has subsidiary rooms at the north-east corner, of which the topmost was certainly, and each of the others probably, a chapel. A modern timber staircase has been erected in the space formerly occupied by these rooms.

The roof turret is rather larger than the others in the castle, and at half height has a small hexagonal chamber from which a narrow flight of steps continues to the summit. A lintel above these steps contains a round hole for the base of a flagstaff, a reminder that this tower was called *Tour de la Banere* — Banner Tower — in the fourteenth century.

Right: This view, from the top of the Eagle Tower, shows the Queen's Tower (Banner Tower) with the Chamberlain Tower beyond. Against the curtain wall between these two southern towers are the foundations of the great hall.

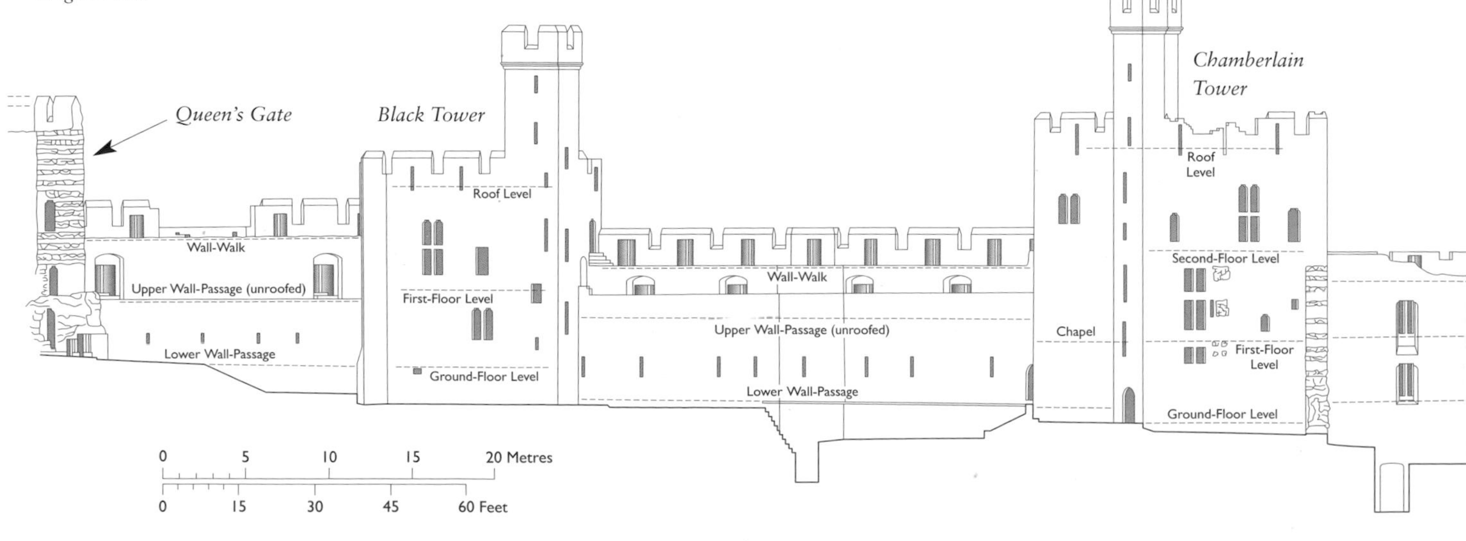

The Great Hall

Against the wall between the Queen's and Chamberlain Towers was the great hall, which was 100 feet (30.5m) long. Although little more than foundations survive, the quality of the masonry at the west (right-hand) end with its fine moulded plinth, shows that, when complete, this must have been a splendid building. The high table would have been to the right, the screens passage, buttery and pantry presumably to the left, where there are now steps leading down to a postern gate. The hall was connected directly to the Chamberlain Tower by a door at the south-east corner.

The Chamberlain Tower

One should enter this tower by the ground-floor entrance signposted for the museum of the Royal Welch Fusiliers. The Chamberlain Tower (also called at different times the Treasury Tower and the Record Tower) is smaller than those previously described and contains three octagonal rooms, each 22 feet (6.7m) wide.

The two lower floors now house the museum of the Royal Welch Fusiliers. Annexed to the north-east angle of each room are small rectangular chambers now used as offices; that on the first floor was formerly a chapel. Continuous wall-passages circle

When complete, the great hall at Caernarfon would have been the scene of lavish entertainment, such as that shown in this thirteenth-century French manuscript illustration, where a king and queen entertain guests at the high table (British Library, Royal Ms. 14 E III, f. 89).

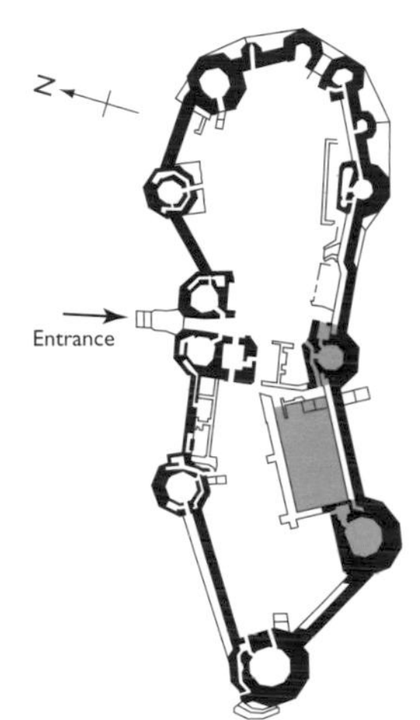

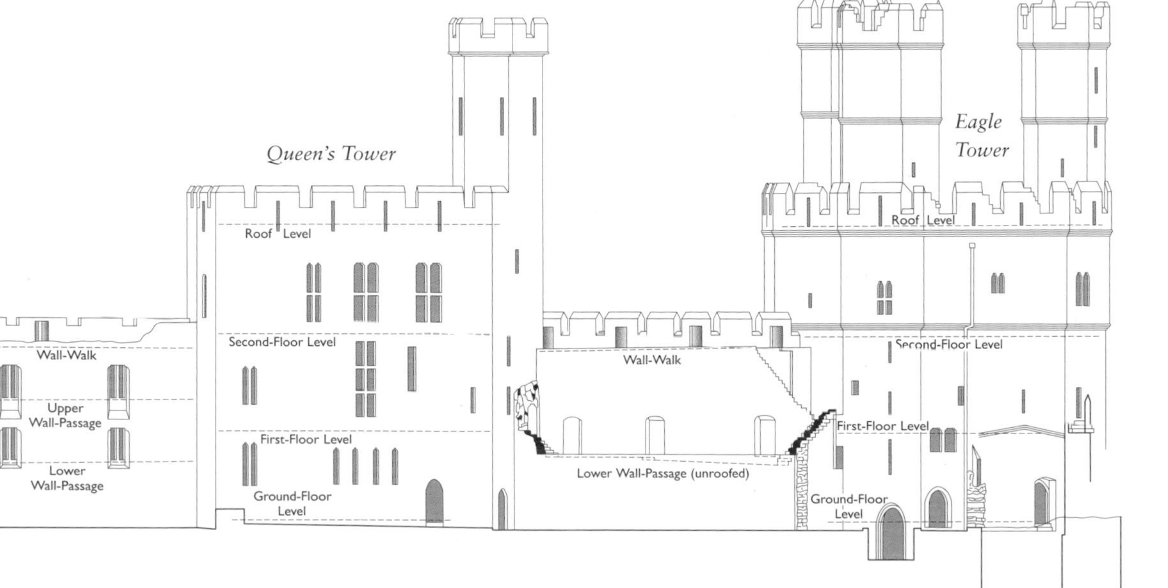

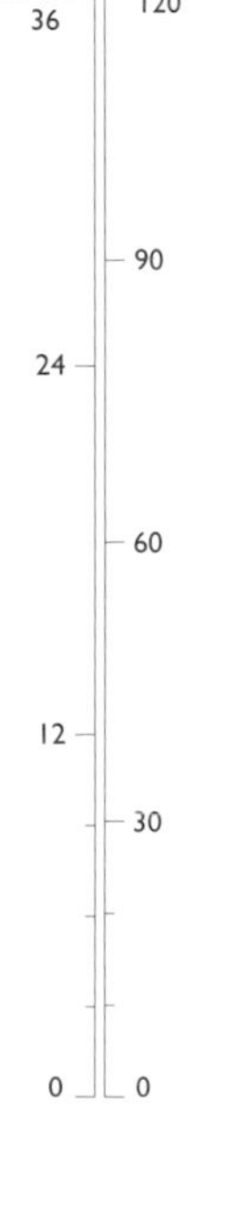

the outer sides of the tower at first- and second-floor levels, which again link with the wall-passages to west and east.

From the second floor, the stair leads to the roof and from there to the top of the turret. The battlements and cresting of the tower proper are original, those of the turret restored. The only surviving stone chimney in the castle is the one on the leads at the back of the turret.

Between the Chamberlain Tower and the Black Tower, the wall-passages continue within the curtain. That on the first floor is now unroofed, but was certainly intended to form a covered gallery like the one below. Above is an open wall-walk at battlement level. The change in direction which the curtain makes midway between the towers arises from the fact that at this point it crosses the line of the ditch of the Norman motte.

A cutaway drawing of the curtain wall as it runs west from the Chamberlain Tower. The drawing gives an indication of the form of the great hall which stood against the wall at this point. The principal arrangements included wall-passages at two levels and a wall-walk above, with the arrangements repeated to the east of the tower. Continuous wall-passages also circle the outer face of the tower itself (Illustration by Chris Jones-Jenkins 1996).

Opposite: The lower wall-passage between the Chamberlain Tower and the Queen's Tower.

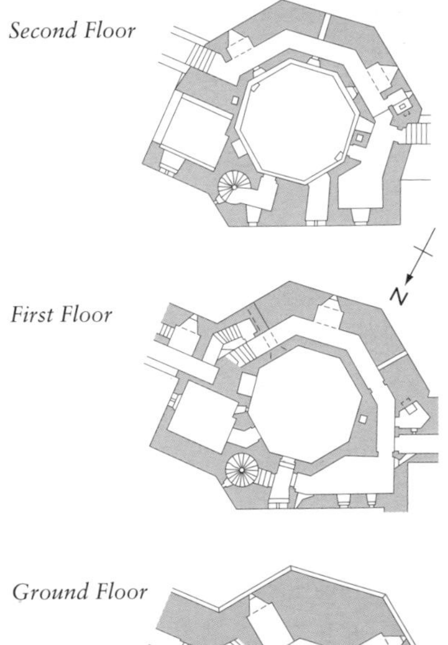

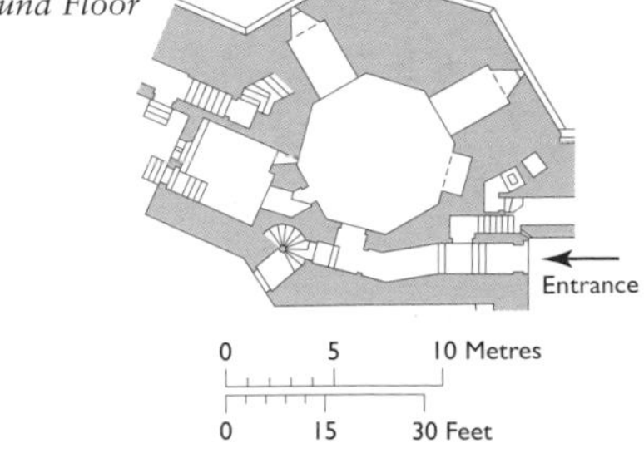

The Black Tower and the Cistern Tower

There is no access at ground level to either of these towers, so to reach them you should enter the doorway to the left of the Chamberlain Tower and make your way along the lower wall-passage. This is the only passage along this part of the wall that does not come to a dead end at the Queen's Gate.

The Black Tower contains two small ten-sided rooms, one above the other, instead of the usual three or four. This was partly because it was built against the side of the motte, so that much of what appears as tower externally is in fact a solid foundation revetting the made ground of the earlier earthwork. There are subsidiary rooms opening off the central chamber at each level, of which the upper, now floorless, consisted of an antechapel with a chapel to the east of it.

The stair in the north-west corner of the tower gives access to this upper floor, to the roof leads and to the surmounting turret. Short flights of steps continue the wall-walk across the leads from one side of the tower to the other, an arrangement not found elsewhere in the castle and it is possible that it was intended to add a third storey to the tower bringing its height up to that of the Queen's Gate. These upper flights of stairs would then have been replaced by a level wall-passage similar to that on the floor below.

As with the Black Tower, a door opens directly from the ground-floor passage into the lower part of the Cistern Tower, which at this level contains a small hexagonal chamber with three arrowloops towards the south. Above the vault there is an open, stone-lined rainwater tank from which the tower takes it name. This can be seen from the wall-walk which may be reached by one of the narrow stairs leading up from the embrasures of the middle (unroofed) passage of the curtain.

A stone outlet channel, which runs through the thickness of the wall and discharges through a shaft in the Queen's Gate, will be noticed crossing one of the nearby arrowloops. The top of the tower appears unfinished and would no doubt have been carried up to match the level of the top of the Queen's Gate.

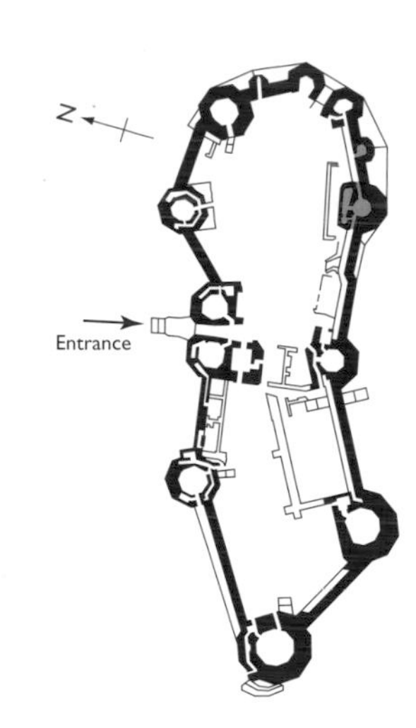

The Black Tower was built with solid foundations against the side of the Norman motte and contains rooms at just two levels.

The cistern, on top of the aptly named Cistern Tower, collected rainwater from the adjacent roofs. Surplus water could be fed by a system of channels to an outlet in the Queen's Gate.

Below: Black Tower (right) and Cistern Tower (left) floor plans.

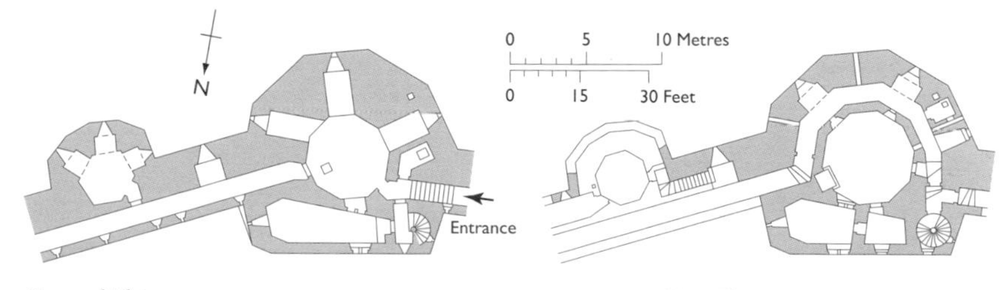

Ground Floor

First Floor

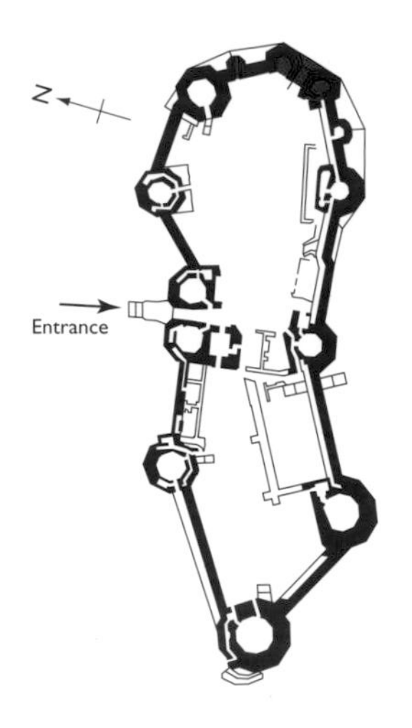

The exterior façade of the Queen's Gate would have originally been approached by a ramp and steps. The elevated position of the gate-passage was dictated by the height of the earlier motte against which the gate is built.

The Queen's Gate

The ground-floor passage from the Cistern Tower leads to the Queen's Gate. This second great gateway was never finished and, seen from within the castle, it can be viewed in 'cross-section'. The unusual character of the external façade, and the elevated position of the gate-passage — high above the street outside — was dictated by the height of the earlier medieval motte, against which this part of the castle was raised. Originally, the gate would have been approached from outside by a great stone-built ramp with gently graded steps.

Seen on plan, the gatehouse consists of a central passage and bridge pit flanked by polygonal towers. At ground level each tower contained an irregularly shaped porter's room, the northern of which still remains open to the courtyard.

The lofty position of this gate made it less vulnerable than the King's Gate and its defences are in consequence less elaborate. There was a

The Castle Accommodation

Whilst traversing the wall-passages, climbing the stairs, and viewing some of the great rooms at Caernarfon Castle, we may well wonder why the castle was built here and on so vast a scale. We may be curious, too, about why so many rooms were provided and who was to use them. The answers are touched upon elsewhere in this guide (pp. 38–39).

We should remember that Caernarfon was to be the capital of a new dominion and the palace of a new dynasty of princes. It had to be capable, when occasion required, of adequately accommodating the household of the king's eldest son, with his council, his family, his guests and all who attended on them. This also implies the capacity to store the treasure, the wardrobe, the records, the provender, the supplies of all kinds required to sustain a great medieval household in appropriate state, as well as to accommodate such officials as the constable and the watchmen, together with a small garrison, whose presence in the castle was a permanency.

History, in the event, seldom if ever fulfilled for the castle the high role intended for it, and in practice, in the fourteenth century at any rate, it had little more to do than serve as the depot for the armament and building maintenance of the other north Wales castles.

In this late fifteenth-century French manuscript illustration, a king and his entourage are seen approaching a walled town. The accommodation at Caernarfon was designed to house such a large royal household when the occasion demanded (British Library, Harley Ms. 4372, f. 79v).

The back of the Queen's Gate, like other parts of the castle, was never completed. It was intended to have porters' rooms flanking the gate-passage and a hall above at first-floor level.

Below: Queen's Gate floor plans.

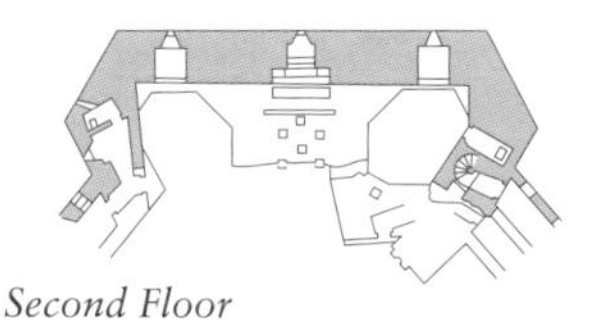

Second Floor

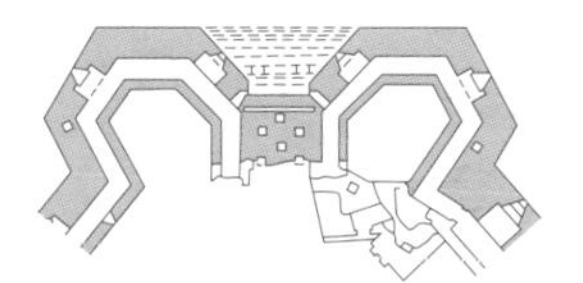

First Floor

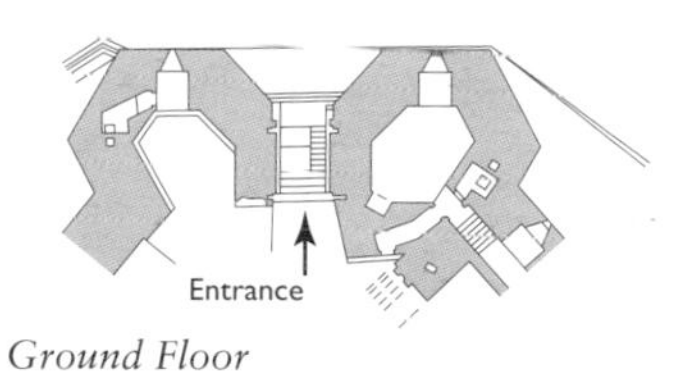

Ground Floor

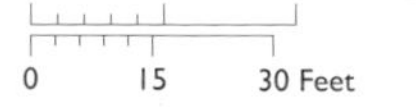

drawbridge (or, more correctly, a 'turning' bridge), and on either side can be seen the bearings for the roller on which it pivoted. Below is a deep pit which took the counterpoise weight when the bridge was in the raised position. Next, there was a portcullis and, above, the vault was well provided with 'murder holes'; you can see six, two of them showing in section towards the courtyard. To the rear of the gate-passage, and slightly to the south of it, an inner gate and portcullis was planned. Above the gate there was to be a wall-passage connecting the passages in the curtain walls to north and south. This can be seen in section on either side where the backs of the gatehouse towers have been left unfinished. At this upper level it was intended that there should be a hall extending, as over the King's Gate, across the full width of the gatehouse.

The Watch Tower

Had the Queen's Gate been completed, the wall-passage in the short section of curtain wall between the gate and the North-East Tower would have connected with the corresponding passage in the south curtain. This passage can only be entered from the North-East Tower. The wall-walk above likewise comes to a dead end at the Queen's Gate.

From the wall-walk a doorway led to the upper part of the slender turret now known as the Watch Tower. The top was a look-out point with a lean-to roof to give cover to the watchman. The battlements both here and on the nearby wall-walk retain traces of the grooves in which were hung wooden shutters for the protection of the crossbowmen.

A section of the battlements on top of the Watch Tower showing one of the grooves in which a wooden shutter was hung for the protection of crossbowmen.

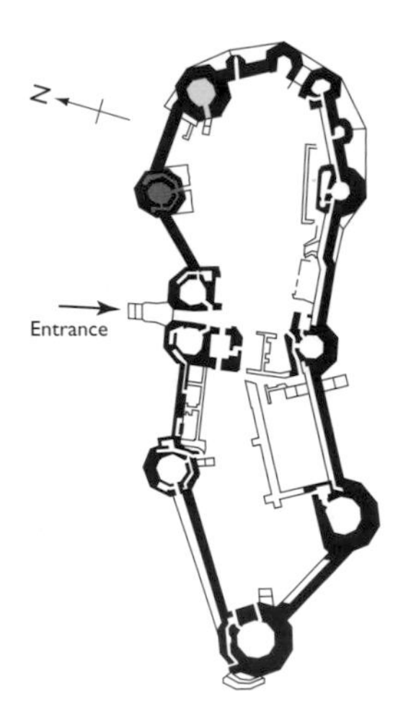

Opposite: Part of the upper ward showing, from right to left, the Watch Tower, the North-East Tower and the Granary Tower. The 'toothing' on the towers indicates that substantial buildings were planned to line the curtain walls, but never built. The curtain wall is notable for its array of multiple arrowloops and the lack of wall-passages compared with its southern counterpart.

The North-East Tower

This is an octagonal tower of two storeys only. The ground-floor room houses an exhibition on the princes of Wales. The characteristic wall-passages of the southern curtain are continued round the outer sides of the tower, but do not go beyond it. This is because the work of the earlier building period terminates here and wall-passages were not provided in the northern curtain which, from this point to the Eagle Tower, dates from 1295 and later. The stair is at the north-west corner and ascends to the top of the turret. The battlements of this turret are unusual in having arrowloops set beneath them.

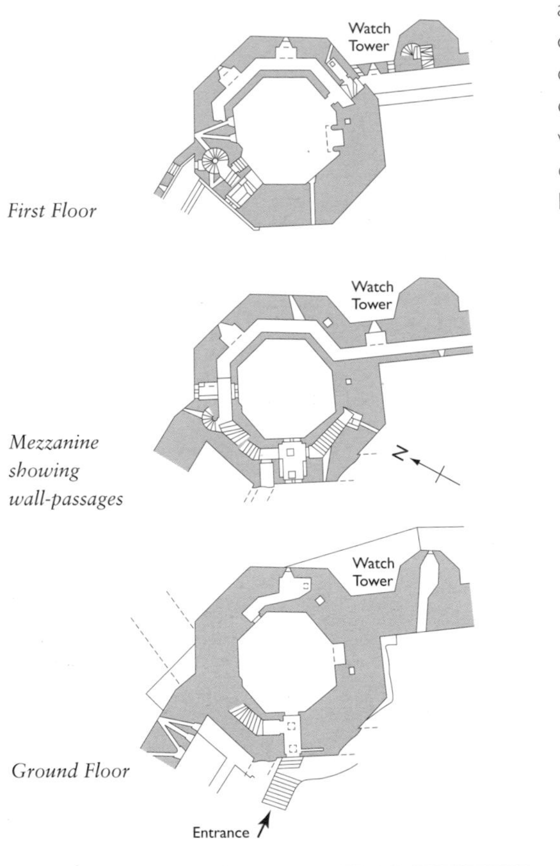

The Granary Tower

In many respects the Granary Tower duplicates the Well Tower. It is octagonal, of four storeys surmounted by a turret, and has a wall-passage at ground level leading to a well chamber. Of the main rooms, only the top floor, which is unroofed, is accessible to visitors. It is crossed by the wall-walk along the top of the curtain which can be followed across the King's Gate to the Well Tower and so down to the courtyard again.

One of the most interesting features in the castle is the multiple grouping of arrowloops at two levels in the curtain wall on either side of the Granary Tower. These represent a refinement of the arrangements noted in the upper floors of the King's Gate (pp. 22–23). The firepower, which these loops enabled to be brought to bear on a limited front, must — by medieval standards — have been devastating.

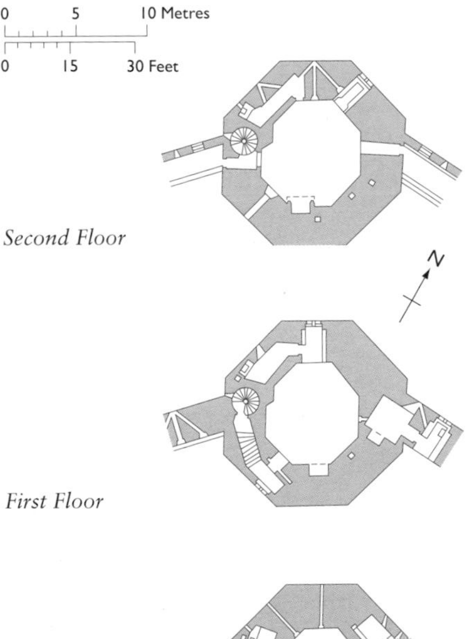

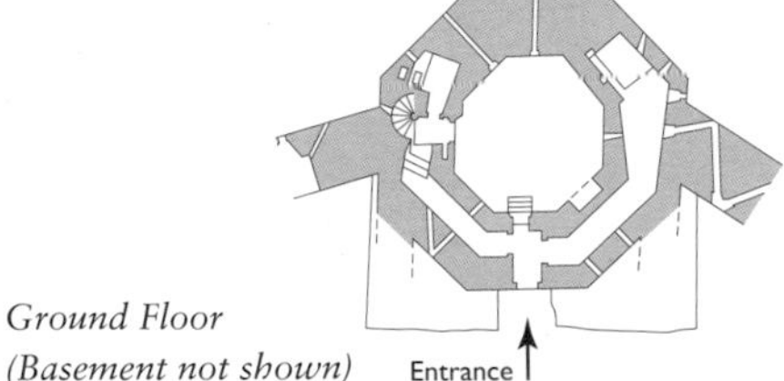

Right. A cutaway section showing how the castle's multiple arrowloops may have been used (Illustration by Chris Jones-Jenkins 1996).

The statue of King Edward II was erected above the King's Gate in 1320.

The North Face of the Castle

Leaving the castle through the King's Gate, note the various defensive features mentioned at the beginning of the tour. Looking back at it from the bridge outside, you will see above the entrance the much weathered statue of King Edward II, the first English prince of Wales. We know the statue was erected in 1320, and it is a reminder that this side of the castle formed part of the second phase of the castle's history. It was raised after the original defences had been overrun during the Welsh revolt of 1294.

The Purpose of the Town and Castle

John Speed's map of Caernarfon shows that the medieval layout had altered little by 1610. The regular street pattern and the borough defences are clear; so too is the King's Pool or mill pond which had been built in 1285. The centre of English administration in north-west Wales, Caernarfon housed a mixed population of administrators, tradesmen, builders and craftsmen (Llyfrgell Genedlaethol Cymru/ National Library of Wales).

When Edward I began to build the walled town of Caernarfon in 1283, and issued its charter of privileges in the following year, his object was to create a nucleus of English influence which could adapt a place famous in Welsh story and with great natural advantages to conditions brought about by the success of his armies. An early draft of the Statute of Wales shows that even before it was decided to form a county of Caernarvonshire, Caernarfon had been selected as the administrative centre for the lands subsequently grouped in the new shires of Caernarvon, Anglesey and Merioneth. The justiciar and chamberlain of north Wales, established to administer the judicial and financial systems of the principality thus annexed to the English Crown, accordingly had their offices in Caernarfon; there the courts were held for the three shires, and there the justiciar had his chief official residence. Within the county organization, the sheriff, the coroners, and other local officers were based there. The new town provided quarters and protection for all these officials, their deputies, clerks and assistants; for the builders and craftsmen who worked on the castle; and for a small maritime and mercantile community who maintained contact with the other English coastal towns in Wales, with England itself through Chester and Bristol, and with the king's possessions in Ireland and Gascony. The rights and privileges prescribed in the charter were intended to attract to a distant and lately hostile land, settlers who, by following these callings, would aid the working out of government policy and the gradual pacification of the country.

Anyone familiar with the other great castles of north Wales — Conwy, Harlech, Beaumaris, Flint, Rhuddlan and Aberystwyth — will have noticed that their round towers give them a certain family resemblance which at Caernarfon is apparent only in the town wall. Here the castle is plainly a building apart, wearing an aspect of nobility all its own. This is chiefly derived from its spacious multangular towers, which must already have been commissioned in 1283, the year in which their foundations were laid. Thus the castle would seem to have been marked

After crossing the bridge, turn right along Castle Ditch. This ditch was originally twice as wide as it is now, and would have isolated the castle from the town. On reaching the angle tower opposite the beginning of the town wall, you will see that the dark bands of stone on the face of the tower stop to its right, marking the change of build between work executed before (to the left) and after (to the right) 1295. At this point, the castle ditch linked to another bordering the town wall and continued past the Queen's Gate to the river Seiont. The town wall proper did not cross the castle ditch, but terminated at its edge, and the smooth vertical face of its upper section can still be seen. From this point a lower and less massive wall was carried down to the full depth of the ditch and across to the castle.

Those not wishing to visit the town walls should turn left after crossing the bridge and make their way along the ditch to the arch in the wall. Shortly before reaching the Eagle Tower, note the break in the coursing of the masonry and the termination of the bands of darker stone which again mark the change of build between work executed before (to the right) and after (to the left) 1295. Beyond the arch lies the river Seiont, to the left, the castle car park.

A section of the ditch west of the King's Gate. Originally much wider, it would have isolated the castle from the adjacent borough.

out for a special role even before the birth, within its precinct, of the first English prince of Wales.

Late in 1285 or early in 1286 the constableship of Caernarfon was granted to the king's closest friend and adviser Sir Otto de Grandison (1238–1328), a Savoyard nobleman from Grandson on Lake Neuchâtel, of whom Edward said, 'there was no one about him who could do his will better'. To this same Otto had already been given the highest appointment of all, that of justiciar of north Wales, a post equivalent to that of viceroy and carrying an annual fee of £1,000. Thus, as soon as its building was well advanced, this particular castle was put in charge of the king's special confidant and lieutenant, who drew the constable's salary of £100 and retained at least nominal custody for the next four years.

We cannot tell how early the decision was taken that the king would eventually confer the principality on one of his sons. Certainly it looks very much as if, at the time the design for the castle was being prepared in 1283, it was already in view as the future official residence of the king's representative in the principality, who, if all went well, would be a prince of Edward's house. Such a purpose would demand a building of specially imposing character — a building which, though fortified with all and more than all the strength of the other castles, might yet have the appearance of a palace. It is most likely for this reason that Caernarfon's towers were not only shaped, but also decorated with broad bands of different-coloured stone, so as to resemble one of the best-known monuments of the Roman empire, namely the city walls of Constantinople.

In 1285–86, Edward I created his closest friend and adviser, Otto de Grandison, constable of Caernarfon. A Savoyard nobleman, Otto was buried in Lausanne Cathedral where his tomb effigy can still be seen (Photograph by Claude Bornand, courtesy of Daniel de Raemy).

The fifth-century walls of the imperial city of Constantinople (modern Istanbul), which provided the inspiration for the walls and towers of Caernarfon Castle (Richard Avent).

THE ANGLESEY

A Tour of Caernarfon Town Walls

The circuit of walls and towers enclosing the medieval borough has survived unbroken. It extends from near the north-east to near the north-west corner of the castle, a distance of about 800 yards (734m). There are eight towers and two twin-towered gateways at intervals of approximately 70 yards (64m).

The North-East Corner of the Castle to the East Gate

From Castle Ditch to the East Gate there are three sections of wall and two intervening towers. Before following Greengate Street along the outside of the wall, turn into Hole in the Wall Street to look at the inside face, where there are the slight remains of one of the stairs which gave access to the wall-walk and to the upper floor of the adjacent tower. The stair has the effect of doubling the thickness of the wall, which is here pierced by a postern gate, formerly closed by a portcullis as well as by wooden doors. Although the inner face of Tower 1 nearby has been stripped, it is still possible to see a sloping line of holes, which show that when it was built an inclined scaffold ramp was used.

Return to Greengate Street, so called because the postern was known as the Green Gate from its proximity to the Green (now Castle Square), and follow it along to Tower 2, which still stands to the full height of the battlements. On either side of it may be seen the fragments of the stone revetment originally built to retain the steep banks which foot the adjoining stretch of wall (the interior of the tower can be seen from an alley off Hole in the Wall Street). The wall from here to the East Gate (3) has been largely refaced with pinkish stone which is more regularly coursed than, and therefore easily distinguishable from, the original masonry.

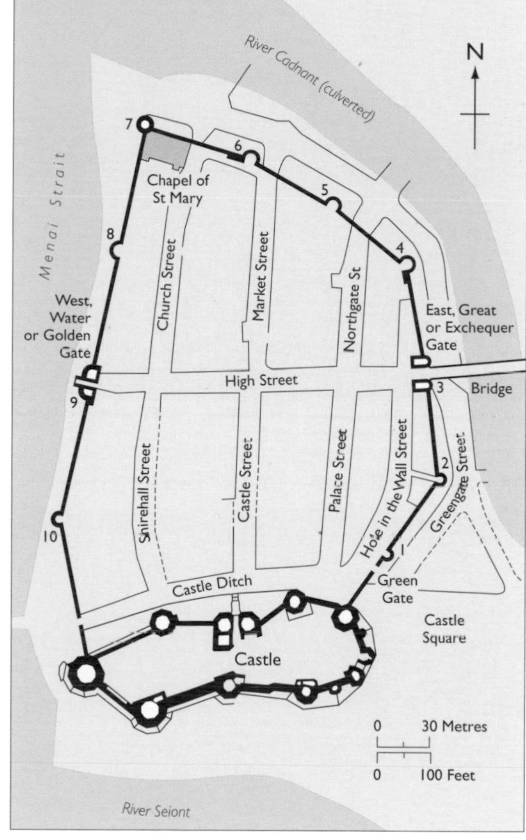

The East Gate

This was the principal landward entrance to the town. Here Greengate Street passes under a stone bridge, which incorporates the final arch of a medieval bridge that was built in 1301 to carry the approach to the walled town across the low-lying river Cadnant (which is now culverted over). It consisted of five stone arches with a timber drawbridge in front of the gate. As this

Opposite: The circuit of walls and towers enclosing the medieval borough survives almost complete. This section, looking along the quay from the Eagle Tower, overlooks the Menai Strait with Anglesey beyond. The twin-towered west gate, known in Welsh as Porth-yr-Aur — meaning Golden Gate, is located midway between the castle and tower 7 in the distance.

The early fourteenth-century seal of the borough of Caernarfon (Society of Antiquaries of London).

Right: The East Gate, also known as the Exchequer Gate, was the main landward entrance into the medieval borough.

Top far right: The section of town wall between Towers 4 and 5 is the best-preserved stretch of the defences.

Bottom far right: In 1303, Edward of Caernarfon licensed Henry of Ellerton to build a chantry chapel in the town of Caernarfon. This marks the foundation of the chapel of St Mary in the north-west corner of the town walls.

A drawing of the East Gate in 1791 by G. J. Farrington. The stone bridge is the last arch of the 1301 bridge that carried the approach road to the medieval walled town across the river Cadnant (Victoria & Albert Museum).

drawbridge was under repair in 1520, it cannot have been replaced by the present stone arch earlier than the sixteenth century. From below, it is possible to see the original width of the bridge, part of which has been exposed to the right beyond the arch. As built in the 1280s, the bridge was a wooden structure; this was destroyed by the rebels in 1294–95, and its rebuilding in stone was put in hand in 1301 or 1302.

In front of the main gate there was originally a smaller, battlemented gateway where the tolls on merchandise were collected; this was connected to the main gate by a drawbridge across the town ditch. The rooms above the main gateway served from the first to accommodate the exchequer, established by the Statute of Wales (1284) as the administrative and financial centre of the counties of Caernarvon, Anglesey and Merioneth. The gateway was altered in 1767 to become the Town Hall, and in 1873 the Guildhall; it incorporates much relatively modern work, but the remains of the twin medieval gate towers can still be seen in their proper relationship to the adjacent walls.

From the East Gate to the Waterfront

Beyond the East Gate is an angle tower (4) standing to the full height of its battlements, which retain their cresting with the remains of finials. The length of wall between this and the next tower (5) is the best preserved of all. Here the battlements contain the bases of arrowloops rising well defined above the level of the wall-walk. The opening to Northgate Street is relatively modern, as are those to Market Street and Church Street. Between Towers 5 and 6 the wall still retains some of the whitening applied to its surface at the back of the buildings which, until the 1930s, entirely screened it from view.

The early fourteenth-century chapel of St Mary is built against the inside of the wall beyond Tower 6; the angle tower (7) is incorporated in it and served as its vestry. Initially, the new borough was served by Llanbeblig church, but in 1303 Edward, prince of Wales, licensed Henry of Ellerton 'to build a chantry chapel in the town of Carnarvan on his burgage there'. The chapel has been much restored, but the arcades are original early fourteenth-century features.

Within the wall, on the opposite side of Church Street, is another of the stone stairs. The inner faces of Towers 4 and 6 are well preserved, together with their bridges, which were originally of timber and subsequently replaced in stone. In 1347 the then chamberlain of north Wales was ordered 'to repair the bridges on the walls of the said town ... so that it may be possible to walk safely on the walls and defend the town in case of peril'. Tower 5, like Tower 1, has lost all its interior facework.

From the North-West Corner to the Castle

The towers on this side of the town are occupied and inaccessible to visitors, but this long stretch of wall facing the Menai Strait still retains its medieval atmosphere in a way that is denied to the parts engulfed by the growth of the later town. Here from the beginning was the quay. Originally it was constructed of wood, but it was burned in the troubles of 1294–95, and was rebuilt in stone in the early fourteenth century.

In the eighteenth century the southern part of what is now The Anglesey was the Custom House.

Just to the south of Tower 7, a blocked doorway is visible. Originally, before the building of St Mary's chapel, a postern gate stood here but the arch was subsequently moved a few feet to form the west door of the chapel. It was blocked up later as a protective measure.

The door, windows, battlements and castellated chimney of Tower 8 are nineteenth-century additions, as are the windows and battlements of the West Gate (9), which consists of a twin-towered gatehouse with a small projecting barbican, and which houses the Royal Welsh Yacht Club. The portcullis grooves still survive in part and there is a fragment of a projecting latrine at wall-walk level just to the left of the left-hand tower. A sixteenth-century record refers to it as the 'Gildyn Yeate' or Golden Gate, and in Welsh it is still the *Porth-yr-Aur*.

Tower 10, which preserves an arrowloop on the left side, is occupied in connection with the adjacent County Offices into which the nineteenth-century buildings of the former County Gaol have been converted. The presence of the Police Station (1853) and the County Hall (1863), the latter containing the Crown Court, recalls the fact that the administration of justice has been carried out on this site for over seven centuries.

The twin-towered West Gate was equipped with a portcullis and could only be approached from the sea in the thirteenth century.

The stretch of town wall facing the Menai Strait was from the outset the town quay and still retains something of its medieval atmosphere.

The best position to appreciate the splendid southern façade of the castle, with its multangular towers and colour-banded walls, is from across the river Seiont.

At the west end of the castle ditch the town wall is pierced by a relatively modern archway on the site of an older and narrower postern, remains of which can be seen to the right of the existing opening. The continuation of the wall from this arch at full height across to the castle was not part of the original plan and dates to 1326. The intention of the thirteenth-century builders was to erect against this side of the Eagle Tower a great Water Gate through which — had it ever been completed — water-borne supplies could have been carried at high tide to the door in the basement of the Well Tower. Note the evidence for this on the left side of the Eagle Tower where there are still to be seen the slot for a portcullis, the springers and jambs of the great arch and two doorways in the face of the tower itself, one above the other. The doors would have provided access to the accommodation above the gate.

Before passing round to the south side of the castle, return to the modern archway and pass through it into Castle Ditch. Just to the left of the Eagle Tower you will see a break in the coursing of the masonry and the termination of the bands of darker stone. This marks the change of build between work executed before (to the right) and after (to the left) 1295.

Returning through the arch and continuing round the Eagle Tower you will pass the entry to the tower basement, with its portcullis groove and strongly barred double doors.

Further along the southern façade, between the Chamberlain and Black Towers, a change in the alignment of the curtain wall marks the position of the ditch which encircled the base of the Norman motte. Indications of the presence of the motte itself appear in the sloping apron or revetment of stone which begins to rise at this point and continues past the Queen's Gate to the North-East Tower. The different angles at which the walls run were governed partly by the existence of this earlier fortification, and partly by the need to provide covering and crossfire over every part of the ground below the castle.

The overall effect of this splendid façade, with its continuous bands of darker-coloured stone, can best be gained by crossing the river.

Further Reading

P. J. Casey and J. L. Davies with J. Evans, *Excavations at Segontium (Caernarfon) Roman Fort, 1975–1979* (CBA Research Report 90, London 1993).

R. R. Davies, *Conquest, Coexistence, and Change: Wales 1063–1415* (Oxford 1987); reprinted in paperback as, *The Age of Conquest: Wales 1063–1415* (Oxford 1991).

T. P. Ellis and John Lloyd, editors, *The Mabinogion: A New Translation*, 2 vols (Oxford 1929), I, 133–50: 'The Dream of Macsen Wledig'.

J. Goronwy Edwards, 'Edward I's Castle-Building in Wales', *Proceedings of the British Academy* **32** (1946), 15–81.

Charles Kightly, *Caernarfon: A Royal Palace in Wales* (Cardiff 1991).

C. R. Peers. 'Carnarvon Castle', *Transactions of the Honourable Society of Cymmrodorion (1915–16)*, 1–74.

Michael Prestwich, *Edward I* (London 1988); new edition (New York and London 1997).

Royal Commission on Ancient and Historical Monuments in Wales and Monmouthshire, *An Inventory of the Ancient Monuments in Caernarvonshire, Volume II: Central* (London 1960), 124–56.

A. J. Taylor, 'The Birth of Edward of Caernarvon and the Beginnings of Caernarvon Castle', *History*, new series **35** (1950), 256–61.

A. J. Taylor, 'The Date of Caernarvon Castle', *Antiquity* **26** (1952), 25–34.

A. J. Taylor, *Caernarvon Castle and Town Wall* (HMSO, London 1953).

A. J. Taylor, 'Castle-Building in Thirteenth-Century Wales and Savoy', *Proceedings of the British Academy* **63** (1977), 265–92.

Arnold Taylor, *Four Great Castles* (Newtown 1983).

Arnold Taylor, *The Welsh Castles of Edward I* (London 1986).